INVESTMENTS

Paul Stegman
2018 Coombsville Rd
Napa, Calif. 94558
253-0072

by Diana Leone

Front cover: Rainbow Geese
Back cover: Lillies and Rolling Stone

© 1982 by Leone Publications
ISBN 0-942786-02-5

First Edition
Published in the United States in 1982 by
LEONE PUBLISHING COMPANY
2721 Lyle Court
Santa Clara, California 95051

Bears Courtesy of Bears In The Wood,
Los Gatos, CA.
Vests sewn on Viking Sewing Machines.
Art Direction: Lauren Smith Design
Photography: Paul Ambrose
Printing: Westwood Press

Dedication

To my friends...all of you, the "group," my customers and my family, who have inspired me, stayed by me and encouraged me to finish.

To all authors who are in print, you understand. To all the publishers who gave me permission to use any of their work.

Especially to the group whom I call friends of the shop; Joan, Diane, Ann, Kelly, Jenny, Sonia, Lanae, Bertie, Eunice, Bobbie, Sondra who put up with me, helped me, and never let me down.

And to Lauren Smith, Art Director who patiently waited and produced this book.

Sincerely,

Diana Leone

Contents

Introduction

Just after Christmas this past year, I found myself sitting around with not much to do. I had planned on publishing the Log Cabin Vest as a single pattern. While I was working on that pattern, my friends used my basic pattern and began creating their own beautiful and unusual vests. What was to take me a month or two as an "in between" project ended up taking over a half year to finish. The simple vest idea grew to what seemed like a fifteen volume set of encyclopedias, including over twenty different vest ideas for children, juniors, and adults, with special emphasis for the mature figure.

As all of our body shapes differ (thank goodness!), I have included easy-to-follow fitting suggestions for that perfect fit.

As you peruse this book, choose a look that fits your personality and style. Be it striking color, fascinating quilting, or a soft, feminine look, decide on one and begin. Each vest has a Thimble Rating on a difficulty scale of one to four—one thimble being easy, four most difficult. The ideas given here are just that, ideas. The format for each vest is a basic flat surface, without darts. You can adapt any design to this pattern, or you can use your favorite pattern and embellish it with any of these ideas. This is just a beginning.

This book is divided into three major methods of sewing.

The first major area is strip or string piecing. Strip piecing comprises of narrow or wide pieces of fabric sewn by themselves or together to form strings of fabric which are sewn to the batting in what we call quilt-as-you-sew.

The first few vests are constructed using the Log Cabin technique. Log Cabins are usually pieced with the first, or center piece placed right side up. The logs or strips are added one by one from the center out by placing each strip face down over the last, sewn through the batting, opened, trimmed and pressed.

Strips are added, usually in a counterclockwise rotation until the batting is filled. These vests include small and large centers. Other strip processes include methods where pieces of fabric are sewn together to form strings. These pieced strings are then sewn to the batting in the quilt-as-you-sew method.

The second area is on hand quilting which includes Sashiko and a short "note on creativity." Machine Applique and Machine Quilting are included in the third area.

If you are familiar with my past work, you will be expecting clear and concise directions. I hope that you find *Investments* worth your time and effort, and that you will create your very own "art-to-wear."

Glossary

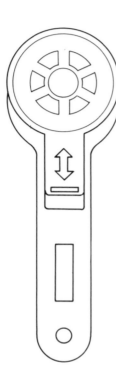

FABRICS

Top-weight or blouse-types of cotton or cotton-polyester blends of even weave were used for most of the vests and are best for the first-time vest maker. The more stable the fabric, the easier it will be to cut it into narrow strips and little pieces. Sheer fabrics, rayon blends, and pile fabrics are best left to the more experienced seamstress.

BATTING

The filler is used to create the textile sandwich and the quilted look. Whatever you use, it would be best to make a practice block unless you are very familiar with the filler. I will use the word batting throughout these instructions because you are using a filler to give the vest a quilted look.

Pellon Fleece®. A thin, dense batting that does not stretch or shift during the quilt-as-you-sew process. Do not pre-shrink Pellon Fleece. I have found that in most cases I can cut this batting exactly the size I need and all will go well. We used this batting for most of the vests in this book.

Other Battings. You may be really familiar with a particular batting. If you like it and understand it, by all means use it. In most cases, a bonded batting is preferred.

Polarguard. We have even used an 8 oz. Polarguard batting for vests to be worn in cold climates. The thicker the batting, the more margin you will need to add for the shrinkage while sewing. Cut thick batting two sizes larger and trim to size after piecing.

Fairfield Ultra Loft. Should be cut two sizes larger than you need. When you are through with the piecing, just reposition your pattern and trim the back and fronts to the size you need. Ultra loft works especially well in the machine quilted projects. (Rainbow)

Flannel. (50% cotton 50% polyester) I have found that a good flannel makes a great batting for a lightweight vest. It hand-quilts beautifully. Pre-shrink before using. Cut the size you need. I also use flannel for a wall covering to lay out my pieces during the designing process.

Muslin. A good muslin also works well. Pre-shrink before using. Cut the size that you need.

CUTTING GUIDES AND TOOLS

Scissors. The single most important tool you will use for all your sewing needs is your scissors. They need to be sharp and well-balanced. At this time I use the Gingher G-8, which is probably the best on the market today, and which will easily cut through six to eight layers at one time.

C-Thru® Ruler, B-85. 2″ (5 cm) x 18″ (45.7 cm), with a ⅛″ (3.2 mm) grid printed on it. You will use this ruler for all phases of patchwork and quilting.

Plexi-glass Strips. Manufactured in a variety of lengths and widths, they are beneficial if you will be doing more strip piecing. They are especially useful when used with the rotary cutter. The 1½″ (3.8 cm) x 22″ (55.8 cm) is the size used for most of the vests in this book.

Rotary Cutter. The *Olfa Rotary Cutter®* is a sharp, round cutting wheel attached to a plastic handle, and is available in two sizes, small and large. Purchase the large size, as it will cut through more layers.

I really like and use this tool. It cuts an incredibly clean line through twenty fabrics at one time. You must be careful, you must read the instructions, and you should practice. If you like good and useful tools, this one is great. The added expenses begin now, since you will need a cutting matt to go with the rotary cutter.

Cutting Matt, Charvoz Cutting Base #49-1136 R. This is a self-healing vinyl cutting matt. You will need some sort of matt to protect any surface if you use the rotary cutter. I have tried every manufactured matt. You get what you pay for. The first one I used lasted about a week. Some were too flexible and created bumps under the fabric. The two sizes that I recommend are: 18″ (45.7 cm) x 22″

(55.8 cm) (will give you an adequate cutting surface), and 22" (55.8 cm) x 36" (91.4 cm), which is the one I prefer.

MARKING TOOLS

Probably the most asked question is, "What pencil should I use?" The answer, of course, depends somewhat on the color of your fabric, and whether the marked line will still show when you are finished. You will probably need different ones for different phases.

Sharpie® Fine Line. Permanent pen for drawing the designs onto the plastic.

Mechanical Drafting Pencil. PENTEL® P-205, 0.5 mm R, for the finest and most accurate markings. Your marked line is your sewing line, and it must be accurate.

The Water Soluble pen may be used for marking your quilting lines, but if you use it on the batting, it may never come out completely. Remove with a spraywater bottle. Do not iron the pen marks.

Borel Veri-thin® Silver Pencil will show up on most dark fabrics (don't use on white fabric). (A sliver of soap works well, too.) Use whatever you can see that will give you a fine line and not show up when you are finished.

NOTE: Test all marking tools for removability before marking the final garment.

THREAD

Use a good, strong sewing thread for your machine piecing. I buy a large spool of a color that is neutral to the entire selection. You can change threads while sewing—this may be necessary when you are working with fabrics with a lot of contrast, such as the full rainbow of colors. I do not like the thread to show in the seam of patchwork, and white would show if used with most fabrics.

Machine embroidery thread is particularly useful for machine applique work. It is finer, has a slight sheen, and will help to keep the machine from troublesome jamming while doing a close satin stitch.

Size 8 Perle Cotton is used for decorative quilting and top stitching.

MACHINE NEEDLES

Use a new needle on your machine when you begin your vest. The needle is the least expensive notion you will need. I change them about every eight hours of sewing. Use a size 70 (10/11) for machine applique and for the majority of your sewing.

HAND NEEDLES

Crewel, size 8, has a large enough eye to be used with a size 8 Perle cotton for your hand stitching around the edges of the vests.

Between, size 8, 9, 10, or 12, may be used for the fine, hand-quilted look.

TEAR-AWAY-STABILIZER

A stiff, paper-like product used between the background fabric and the feed dog when doing machine applique. It stabilizes the fabric to eliminate puckering, and you tear it away when you are finished.

PLASTIC SHEET

A thin, stiff, clear plastic used for template making. Cuts easily with scissors. Use the permanent Sharpie fine point pen for marking.

PATTERN PAPER

Any large sheets of paper to make a separate pattern.

THIMBLE

Necessary for any handwork. Metal, leather, plastic, any kind, but you need one for all handwork of any duration.

FLANNEL

One and a half yard piece of white flannel pinned to a wall for a design surface. I use a flannel wall for almost all of my pieced design work. The little cut pieces of fabric will adhere to the flannel and you can move them around to finalize your design. Pellon® fleece works well as a "flannel board."

SEWING MACHINE

Well-cleaned and happy. Zig-zag stitch needed for machine applique.

SEWING MACHINE ATTACHMENTS

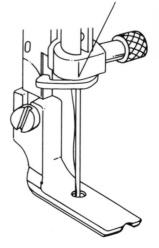

Open-toe Foot. Metal machine foot designed to give you proper tension for machine applique. You can see your satin stitch while sewing. Manufactured for most machines, high and low shank.

Cording Foot. Used to sew cording inside bias. Grooved underneath to hold the cording.

Zipper Foot. Used for under stitching the seam allowance to lining at the armholes. Also used to sew close to covered cord when applying to an edge.

Quilting Guide. An attachment used as a guide to sew parallel lines.

CORDING
Twisted, flexible cord used inside bias for a corded finish around vest edges. Size 16.

UNDERSTITCHING
Method used to sew armhole seams to the lining. The seam allowances are held with the lining and stitched close to the seam. Used when a bound edge is not preferred. The zipper foot is used to stitch close to the seam.

CLEANING
Dry cleaning is recommended. If you have pre-shrunk your fabrics you may hand wash your vest.

FABRIC GLUE STICK
An adhesive used to glue the edges of the applique pieces to the outer fabric for machine applique. It washes out.

GRAIN LINES
Lengthwise with selvage edge, usually printed straight. Crosswise, selvage to selvage, usually not printed straight. Bias, cut 45° from cross wise to lengthwise. Used for binding and cording because it is flexible.

QUILT-AS-YOU-SEW
A technique used for sewing patchwork and strips directly to the batting. This technique is used for most of the vests in this book.

PRESSING CLOTH
A piece of muslin, 12" (30.5 cm) x 12" (30.5 cm), used damp for pressing.

SPRAY BOTTLE
Filled with water, used for misting while pressing.

IRON
Used with a pressing cloth. Do not use the steam as it may leave unwanted spots on your fabric.

Getting Started

APPROXIMATING YARDAGE REQUIREMENTS

The yardage requirements listed for each vest are ample.

To visualize what you will need, lay the pattern out on paper at home. The store will love you if you go in prepared, and you may even save some money.

If you do a layout at home, you will see that you will be able to use some of the leftover lining fabric for the outer work. Cut the lining only after you have done your final fitting of the batting.

I do not like to recommend buying pieces of less than one-fourth (.23 m) yard. You may only need one cut strip, but you need the extra fabric to compensate for shrinkage and off-grain printing. Childrens' sizes will, of course, take less, and in many cases may be made from the leftover fabrics from the adult vests. Linings will vary, but generally three-fourths (.68 m) of a yard will be enough for sizes 8–14 while one and a half yards (1.4 m) will be needed for the sizes 16–22 and one-half yard (.46 m) for the childrens sizes.

FABRIC SELECTION

Careful fabric selection for your vest is essential. You must like the fabrics in order to enjoy sewing with them.

I find that choosing one fabric that I really like is the easiest way to begin. In many cases I fall in love with a particular fabric and then do my designing. The entire vest may be created around one piece of fabric that I like.

If the fabric has two or more colors plus white, I call it a "blender" because it is easier to mix or blend with a greater variety of fabrics. A blender is especially useful as the beginning fabric when selecting for the random string work.

Be brave. Go to your favorite fabric shop and explain to the staff which vest you are making. Decide on your favorite color range. If it is blue, for instance, select a blue fabric that you like. This first fabric will give the person helping you a "clue" or color key. Take your bolt of fabric off the shelf and hold it across many other bolts. Some of these fabrics will come forward and begin to look good with your first choice. Take many bolts off the shelf. You may need only four or eight, but it is easier to choose from a wide range than from a limited palette. It is like a painting. The more variety you have, the more blending you will be able to do. Blues, for example, go to yellow, green, red and grey. There is a big difference, but your eye will do a lot of blending for you and make colors become what you want. When you look at your fabrics, try to look at narrow pieces.

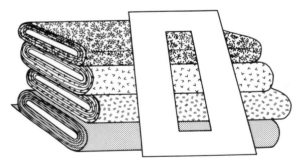

You can cut a long narrow slit in a piece of paper and hold it over the fabrics to give you a better idea of how the narrow strips will actually appear when sewn together. Fabrics are usually printed parallel with the selvage. The printing is seldom parallel with the width, that is, straight with the cross grain of the fabric. Some stripes or plaids may need to be cut individually, but, generally speaking, your strips will be so narrow that the printing will not interfere with the finished appearance of the garment. Always cut your fabrics, since tearing weakens the fabric along the seam, pulls the threads, and wastes fabric and money.

Vests take very little fabric to make. The total cost is small compared to the end result. Now is not the time to sacrifice quality. Buy the best fabrics you can find. It will be your best investment.

The gals in my shop take great pride in helping the customer select fabrics. Our main objective is to give you the confidence to do it on your own. We want you to be proud of what you make and wear.

FABRIC PREPARATION

It is always best to pre-shrink your fabrics. Wash in a short, gentle cycle, using cool water. Hot water and a hot dryer will set the wrinkles into the fabric. When you dry your fabrics, place a large, dry towel in the dryer with the fabric. The towel will act as a buffer and absorb the moisture quickly. Your fabrics will be almost dry in just a few minutes. Remove the fabrics before they are completely dry. Place them on a flat surface and smooth them out. Press as needed.

It is definitely easier to do any handwork on pre-washed fabrics. If you should decide ahead of time that your vest is going to be dry cleaned, then take a day or two and send your fabric to the dry cleaners before you sew. Ribbons and lace shrink a lot, as much as four to six inches to the yard. You may pre-shrink these by hand; wash them by hand in the sink and lay them out to dry on a flat surface. If they need pressing, wrap them in a damp towel to moisten. Press them while damp, using a pressing cloth.

I have spent the better part of the past six months working on all the phases of this book so that you would be able to choose a vest and make it in a few hours or days, so let me share some thoughts with you.

First of all, most of the techniques included in this book *are* easy; some of the vests, like the random string vest, should take you about three hours from cut to finish.

You will spend more time carefully selecting your fabric than you will actually spend sewing your garment. Don't belabor the techniques. Make a practice block or sample if you are not familiar with the technique, such as machine applique. But if you are fairly secure, just dig right in.

QUILT-AS-YOU-SEW

All of your piecing and quilting will be done on a batting or filler to create a "quilt-as-you-sew" garment. If the batting fits, the finished vest will usually fit. You will merely need to select your size, place the batting over the pattern, trace the two fronts and the back,

baste together using a ½″ (12 mm) seam, and try it on.

Of course, the batting and fabric will shrink somewhat—depending on the stability and thickness of the batting and the number of seams. Pellon Fleece®, or similar batting, will be the most stable. We used Pellon Fleece® for most of the vests. Fairfield Ultra Loft® was used for the machine quilted vests. The more seams you sew, such as in the strip vests and the gridpieced vests, the more the batting and vest will shrink.

A walking foot, or dual feed foot, is a tremendous help in the "quilt-as-you-sew" method. Lots of folks are not familiar with it, and think it is a nuisance to have this large attachment in the way. If you do try one, you will use it more than you ever dreamed possible. This foot feeds the top fabric evenly with the bottom fabric so that when you get to the end of a seam the fabrics are still even on the bottom and top. When using the dual feed foot for sewing the strip piecing onto the batting, it literally eliminates the loss of inches. (It may be safer for you as a beginner to just cut the batting larger than needed. You can always trim it to size after you have pieced.)

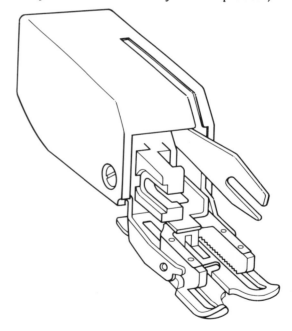

But what happens, then, to the hand quilted ones? If you cut these larger and quilt all the way to the edge, you will cut all of your threads when you trim it to size. Sure, these threads will be caught in your machine-sewn seams, but some careful handling will be necessary. If you use thin batting the vest will remain the finished size. Stitch to and through the seam allowance and sew the vest together.

This vest pattern fits the majority of body shapes. I do not want it to gap in the back, or to be loose in the armholes, so I have included some easy fitting instructions. I have tried to include designs for the mature figure. So many ladies who are larger sizes have come into the shop because they wanted to wear some unobtrusive yet beautiful vest and could not find it in ready-to-wear. I also have had many requests for a child's pattern, but more than that, one for the preteen or junior. I have found that the juniors will wear a vest if it is not too cute and if they feel comfortable in it. We all remember those years. Also, one may say that she doesn't want to put a lot of work into a growing child's garment. To heck with that! That would be like saying put a sack over them 'till they grow up. What time and effort you do put into your work will be well rewarded with smiles and compliments, even if for only a short time. I hope you will be able to sort this all out and jump right in!

Making and Fitting the Trial Vest

MEASURING THE PATTERN

All of the patterns are "graded," that is, each pattern is actually sewn ½″ (12 mm) smaller than the cut size. Measure the pattern under the armhole from seam line to seam line, which is ½″ (12 mm) from the edge of the pattern since a ½″ (12 mm) seam allowance is included in the pattern.

NOTE: You may find that you have a size 10 front and a size 12 back. It is all right to interchange the patterns—each body is individual.

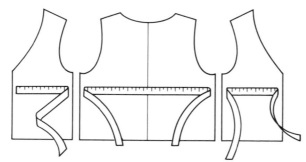

FITTING FOR THE MATURE FIGURE

Some of you may need to make some slight adjustments. If you have ever taken a tailoring class and had to make a fitted vest, you will remember that the vest had a center back seam. This is where the pattern was adjusted to fit the curve of the back. It was as simple as that. In your "art-to-wear" vest, there can be no center back seam, since it would eliminate the flat surface needed for the design area. If you need to make some adjustments in the fit, you will have a center back seam on the batting only.

CUTTING AND FITTING THE BATTING

Select your size from the pattern folded into the back of the book. Place the batting over the pattern. You should be able to see the pattern through the batting. Trace the back and two fronts. If you can't see through the

Selecting Your Size

Measure your bust and add 3″ (7.6 cm)

(1) Size	(2) Bust	+3″ (7.6 cm) for ease	(3) Pattern should measure from seam line to seam line
8	30″ (76.20 cm)		33″ (83.82 cm)
10	32″ (81.28 cm)		35″ (88.90 cm)
12	34″ (86.36 cm)		37″ (93.98 cm)
14	36″ (91.44 cm)		39″ (99.06 cm)
16	38″ (96.52 cm)		41″ (1.05 m)
18	40″ (1.02 m)		43″ (1.09 m)
20	42″ (1.07 m)		45″ (1.15 m)
22	44″ (1.12 m)		47″ (1.19 m)

Write measurements here:

Size _____ Bust _____ , plus 3″ (7.6 cm) ease _____ = pattern _____ .

Length, back neckbone to desired finished length _____ .

Always go for the next larger size. It is easier to trim than to add.

batting, make another pattern out of paper. The pattern has some of the placement lines for your particular view marked on it. (Each view is marked with a coded line.)

- Trace the placement lines onto your batting.
- Cut out the batting for your size.
- Pin and baste the side and shoulder seams together, using a ½" (12 mm) seam which is included in the pattern.

(NOTE: To baste by machine, loosen the top tension on your machine to about 2 (5 is normal). Use the longest stitch on your machine. This will make the underside stitch loopy and easy to remove later by pulling out the bobbin thread.)

Try it on. Be sure that you try it on with the seams *on the inside,* or you will reverse any adjustments.

For most of you, the batting will fit well at this time. If so, remove the basting stitches by pulling out the bobbin thread, and continue on with the instructions for your vest.

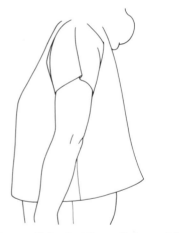

If the hem of the batting sticks out in the back, slit the center back up to the fullest point between the shoulders. Overlap the batting at the hem until the gap is gone.

- Top stitch down the center back by hand or machine. Trim the excess batting.
- The batting will have a slight hump across the shoulders, but this will not interfere with the surface design.

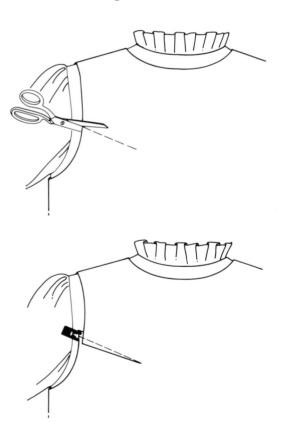

- If the armhole or neck back does not lay smoothly, make small darts following the same procedure as with the back. Just slit the batting, overlap, and top stitch.

NOTE: Remember, these fitting suggestions may seem a bit involved (and for most of you won't be necessary), but if you need to adjust for fit, this will do it.

CHECKPOINTS FOR FITTING

Shoulder adjustments

Your own two shoulders may vary. Try on the batting *right side out* so that you won't reverse the adjustments.

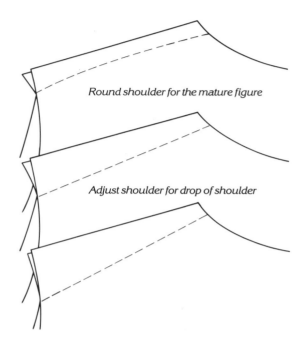

Round shoulder for the mature figure

Adjust shoulder for drop of shoulder

Length

The vest is about 3″ longer than the average waist. To lengthen or shorten just add or subtract on the paper pattern.

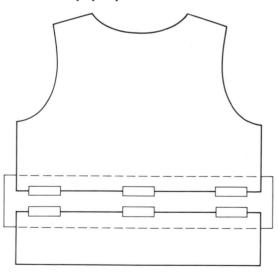

Fronts

The vest is designed to not close in the front. If you need to add for the full figure, just cut a strip of batting and add a strip to each front. Add one inch to each front for each size larger than 20. If the batting is thin you may overlap and topstitch. If the batting is thick just "butt" the edges of the batting together and hand whip.

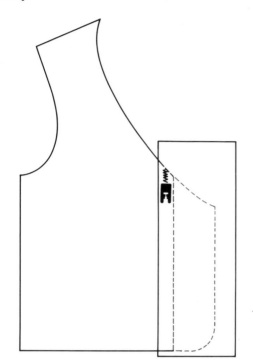

If the batting vest fits, remove basting stitches. Note on your pattern all revisions that you have made in the batting vest. I work directly with the batting. It is inexpensive and similar in weight to the finished garment. Do not pre-shrink the batting; it is unnecessary.

Stack Cutting

Stack cutting is a method of layering folded fabrics and cutting through as many layers as your tool will permit. Many tools on the market make stack cutting easier. Refer to Cutting Guides and Tools, page 6, for scissors or rotary cutter information.

PREPARING TO CUT
- Be sure to set aside any fabrics needed for center squares so that they do not get cut into strips.

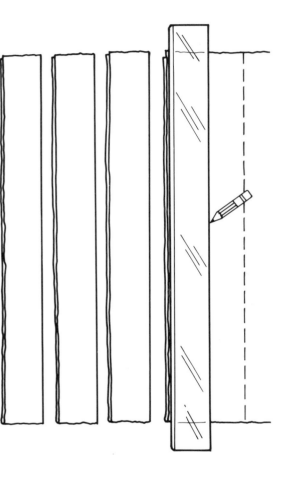

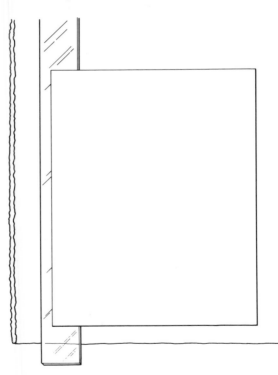

- Fold the pre-shrunk fabric in half, selvage to selvage, right sides together. Stack the fabrics on top of each other, with the folded edge toward you. I like to place the fabric with the lightest color on the top so that it will be easier to see the marked lines.
- Place your cutting guide on the top fabric about one inch from the raw edges. Use a piece of paper as a L-square to align your cutting guide.

- Make sure that wherever you mark you will be cutting through all the layers. Do not worry about this waste; it has been figured into the yardage requirements.
- Mark the number of widths needed. Place your marking tool close to your marking guide. Be consistent and careful, any variation at this time will affect your finished product. The cut edge will be your sewing guide.
- The strip width varies for the different vests. Refer to your particular style for the width requirements. The width required includes the ¼″ (6 mm) seam allowance needed on either side of the strip.

CUTTING

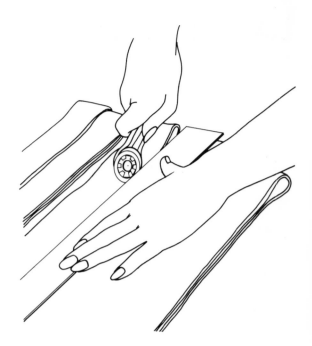

- Hold your scissors or rotary cutter perpendicular to the cutting surface. Cut cleanly and carefully. Cut all of your strips now. You will have more than you need, but you can use them on another project. If you are using the rotary cutter and cutting board, follow the manufacturer's directions.

- Trim off the selvages while you have the stacks together.
- Refer to your vest for further instructions.

Lining the Vest
Method 1

There are three basic methods used for lining the vests. Each vest refers to one of these three methods.

I enjoy using unusual linings. Following the Japanese philosophy used in kimono making, the lining should be as interesting as the outer garment. It may be a splashy contrast or very subtle. Whatever you choose, have fun with it.

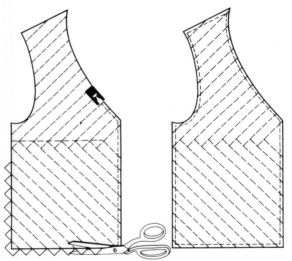

- Trim the fabric and batting of the finished vest parts to the original pattern size:

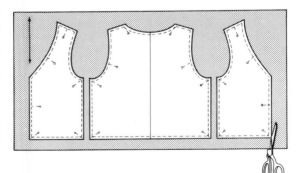

- Use the trimmed vest parts as the pattern: place these parts with the lining fabric, right sides together, and mark the cutting lines. Cut out the lining.

- Sew the outer vest fronts and back together at the shoulder seams. Use a ½" (12 mm) seam, which is included in the pattern.
- Sew the lining fronts to the lining back at the shoulder seams. Use ½" (12 mm) seam.

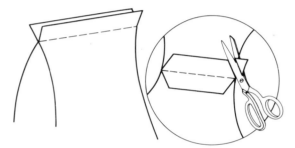

- Trim seams as shown to remove extra bulk.
- If you are using button loops or ribbons for closures, baste them in now to the right front.
NOTE: If you are adding cording to the edges, stop here and refer to: The Corded Edge or Trim, page 20.

Button Loops

The button loops are mainly for decoration—the vests are not usually buttoned. I like to use unusual buttons as jewelry (notice the candy hearts and the ball and jacks). On these vests I add the loops. Sometimes, for fun, I make the loops of different colored fabric to match the change in colors on the vest.

- You will need 4 loops, each 3" (7.6 cm) long. Cut a strip of fabric 1½" (3.8 cm) wide by 18" (45.7 cm) long. Fold strip in half lengthwise, right sides together. Sew down the middle of the strip, ⅜" (10 mm) from fold.

- To turn the loops cut a V-shaped notch ½" (12 mm) from one end of strip. Place a long bobby pin into and through the strip, turning it right side out. Remove bobby pin; trim end. Cut 4 loops, 3" (7.6 cm) long. Press.

- Fold the loops end to end, matching cut edges. Pin loops onto the vest right front, matching dots on pattern (remember, if you have to lengthen or shorten the vest, adjust loop spacing accordingly).
- Baste loops ¼" (6 mm) from edge of the right front.

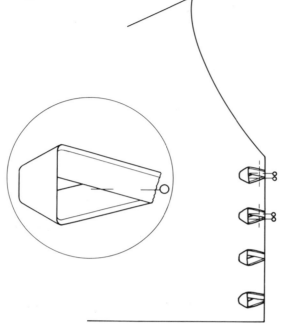

Sew the Lining to the Vest
- Place the outer vest and vest lining right sides together and pin closely around all vest edges except the side seams.
- Sew ½" (12 mm) from these pinned edges, beginning at the center of the back neck edge, and continuing around the front and bottom of the front.
- Remove the vest from the machine and go back and sew from the center neck back down the other front and bottom.

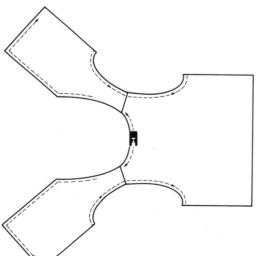

Making the Side Seams Match
- Fold the vest at the shoulders and place the side seams together. Pin the top of the armholes exactly together. With side seams together, notice where the front stitched seam line is at the bottom. (You haven't sewn the bottom back seam yet.) Mark exactly where you need to sew the back bottom seam. If you take a moment to match this seam line up with the one already sewn, it will match when you sew the side seams together, and the vest will be a snap to turn right side out.

- Sew the bottom back seam line.
- Sew the armholes ½" (12 mm) from edges.

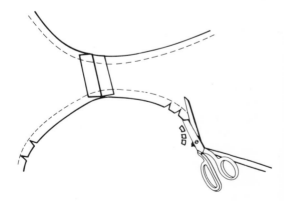

- Clip the curved seams every ¼"–½" (6 mm–12 mm). Clip carefully right up to the seam line. Take a moment and do it right.
- Now trim all the sewn seams to ⅛" (3.2 mm) so that when you do the hand-quilting around the edges the seams won't be bulky.

Turning the Vest Right Side Out

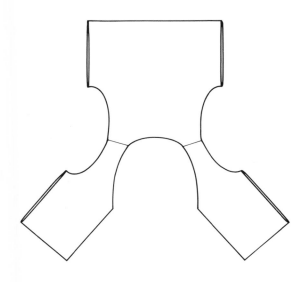

- Reach through one back side opening to the shoulder seam. Begin pulling one front through the inside by easing the bulk at the shoulder seam through first. Poke the corner of the vest front up to the shoulder seam area and grab it with the hand that is already there. Pull the vest front through the back side opening. Reach through the SAME BACK SIDE OPENING and grab the other vest front. Ease it through its shoulder seam area and pull it through. Use a crochet hook or a chopstick and poke any corners out.
- Press all the edges, using a damp pressing cloth.

Side Seams
- With the right sides together and raw edges even, pin the vest lining at the sides. Match the armhole seams and lower hem seams.

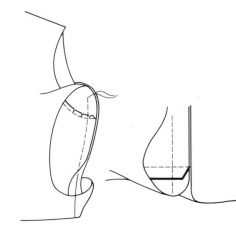

- Begin stitching 2″ (5 cm) above armhole seam in the lining fabric.
- Stitch the vest side seam and continue stitching 2″ (5 cm) of lining below hem seam.
- Press seam open. Trim. Sew the other side seam.
- Trim inside seam allowances of the remaining lining edges.
- Press and pin.
- Hand sew the lining side seams together using a fine blind hem stitch.

- Stitch around the outer edges of the vest by hand. Use a matching thread or size 8 Perle cotton and top stitch around the edges as close as you can without going through the bulk of the seams. About ¼″ (6 mm) from the edge. A balloon wrapped around the point of your needle will help you grip the needle to pull it through the bulk.
- Sew on the buttons and wear it!

19

Lining the Vest

Method 1A—The Corded Edge or Trim

Materials

	CHILD 8–10	JUNIOR 5–9	ADULT 8–14	ADULT 16–22
Cord, size 16	2 yd (1.8 m)	2 yd (1.8 m)	3 yd (2.7 m)	3 yd (2.7 m)
Bias, cut 1″ (2.5 cm) wide	2 yd (1.8 m)	2 yd (1.8 m)	3 yd (2.7 m)	3 yd (2.7 m)
Fabric	½ yd (.46 m)	½ yd (.46 m)	½ yd (.46 m)	½ yd (.46 m)

NOTIONS:
Piping or Cording foot, zipper foot.
Matching thread.

REFER TO:
1) Lining the Vest Method 1, page 17.
2) Continuous Bias for Binding, page 23.
(I know this will be more covered cord than you need, but it is so much fun to make I know you will find another use for it!)

If there is no cording foot for your machine, you may use a zipper foot.

MAKING THE COVERED CORD

NOTE: if you are using a zipper foot to cover the cord do not try to sew too close to the cord the first time around.

You will sew a little bit inside your first stitched line when you sew the cord to the vest. When you sew the lining to the vest you will sew slightly inside that stitching line. If you sew it this way the cord will get tighter each time you sew, you will have a nice line to follow and no stitching will show.

• Cut bias 1″ (2.5 cm) wide. Fold the bias in half right side out. Place the cord inside the fold.

• Using the cording foot, sew the cord into the bias. The seam allowance when finished should be close to ¼″ (6 mm). If it is not, trim it.

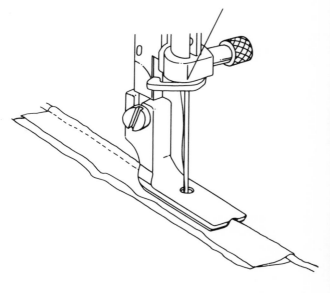

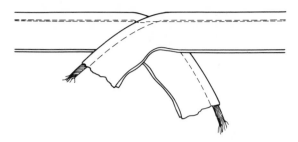

- Leave the cording foot on the machine. Begin at an armhole side seam, align the raw edges of the covered cord with the raw edge of the vest, RIGHT SIDES TOGETHER, and sew cording to armhole, ½" (12 mm) from the edge.
- Sew the cord to the other armhole.

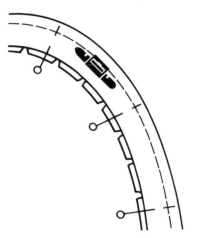

- Refer to your style to see where else you will sew cording.

- Overlap the two ends of the covered cord to create a nicely finished edge.
  You may take out a few stitches and remove the cord from the inside to eliminate the bulk.
- Sew straight across the cross-over by machine.
- Refer to page 18, sew the lining to the vest to finish.
- Pin the lining to the vest (basting would be nice).
- Put the zipper foot on the machine.
- Beginning at the right bottom side front, sew the lining to the vest. You will follow the stitches made by sewing the cord to the vest.

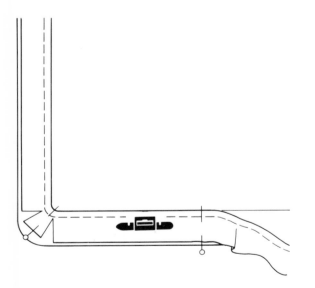

- If all the edges are to have a corded finish, begin at the left bottom side front and sew cording to the first point or curve.
- The bias cord MUST be clipped at the points and curves in order to turn nice corners.
- Sew exactly to the corner; lift the presser foot and clip the bias; turn the vest; lower the foot; continue sewing.
  HINT: If you have a free-arm sewing machine, bend the fabric and the cord down the front of the arm to add a little tension.

Lining the Vest
Method 2

Some of the vests look better if the fronts and hem are bound with bias fabric and the armholes are not bound. The armhole may be understitched by machine to hold the seam allowances to the lining, or the armhole seam allowances may be turned in and hand sewn. (Bias lesson is included in this chapter.)

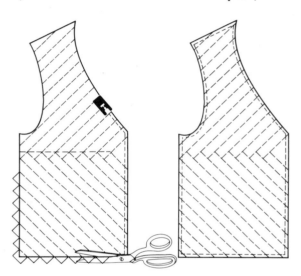

- Trim the fabric and batting to the original vest pattern size. Stay stitch around all edges ¼" (6 mm) from edge.

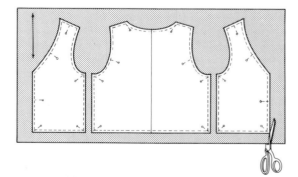

- Cut out the lining from the pattern, or use the outer vest pieces as a pattern and place them with the lining, right sides together. Pin and cut out the lining.

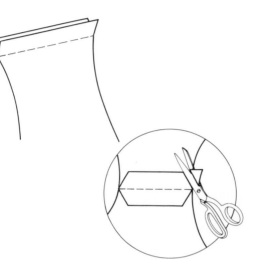

- Sew the vest fronts and back together at the shoulder seams, using ½" (12 mm) seam.
- Pin the vest lining fronts to the back at the shoulder seams; sew with ½" (12 mm) seam.
- Press shoulder seams open. Trim.

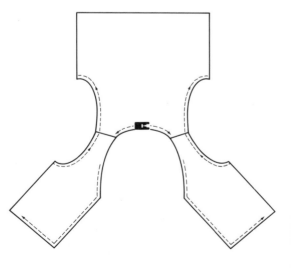

- Pin the lining to the outer vest, right sides together, around all raw edges.
- Sew around the armholes by machine, using ½" (12 mm) seam.

- Clip the armhole curves every ¼″ (6 mm) to the seam line. Trim the armhole seams to ¼″ (6 mm).

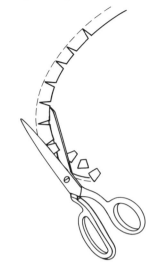

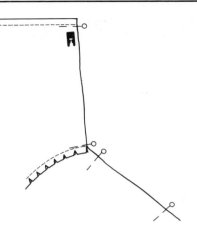

UNDERSTITCHING

- Use zipper foot.
  Holding the lining away from the outer vest, push the seam allowances toward the lining and top stitch, beginning at the shoulder seam, through the lining and seam allowances as close as possible (⅛″ (3.2 mm)) to the armhole seam. Sew to the side seam. The stitching will appear on the lining only.
- Go back and sew from shoulder seam to side seam. You will reposition the zipper foot when you sew in the opposite direction in order to sew close to the seam.

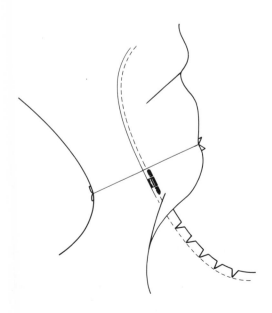

- Sew the side seams. With right sides together and raw edges even, pin vest and lining at sides; matching armhole seams.
- Sew together using ½″ (12 mm) seams.
- Bind all outer edges with bias. Cut the bias 3″ (7.6 cm) wide.

NOTE: Some of the vests were staystitched around the armholes and not bound around the edges. If this is the look you want, do not sew the armholes closed yet, just staystitch and go back to method 1, page 17.

CONTINUOUS BIAS FOR BINDING

For most of the vests, a 3″ (7.6 cm) wide bias folded in half will make a good width for the binding. You may wish to vary the width.

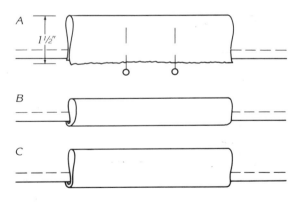

To determine how wide you need to cut the binding, just take a strip of a scrap approximately 3″ (7.6 cm) wide by 5″ (12.7 cm) long.

- Fold this test piece in half.
- Pin the two raw edges of the piece to an edge of the vest, using ½″ (12 mm) seam allowance.
- Bring the fold to the back and see how it looks. Should be fine. Make any width adjustments now.

23

Bias Binding Materials

	Number of yards of binding cut in widths				
	1" (2.5 cm)	1½" (3.8 cm)	2" (5 cm)	2½" (6.4 cm)	3" (7.6 cm)
½ yard of fabric (18" sq. or 116 cm²)	7½ yd (6.86 m)	5 yd (4.5 m)	4 yd (3.6 m)	2½ yd (2.29 m)	1½ yd (1.4 m)
¾ yard of fabric (27" sq. or 174 cm²)	18 yd (16.4 m)	12 yd (10.9 m)	9 yd (8.2 m)	7 yd (6.4 m)	5 yd (4.57 m)

Measure around your vest where you need binding. Find the width and length you need on the chart. You will probably make more than you will need, but you will have some left to practice cording or bias.

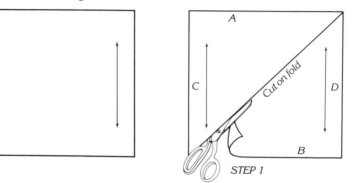

STEP 1

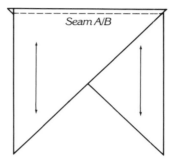

STEP 2
- *Place A and B right sides together.*
- *Sew A and B together.*
- *Overlap points of A and B and sew ½" seam allowance.*

STEP 3
- *Place L-Square or yardstick on the inside of the fabric and mark desired finished CUT width.*
- *Move L-Square and mark again.*
- *Connect marks with straight line.*

STEP 4
- *Bring C and D together*

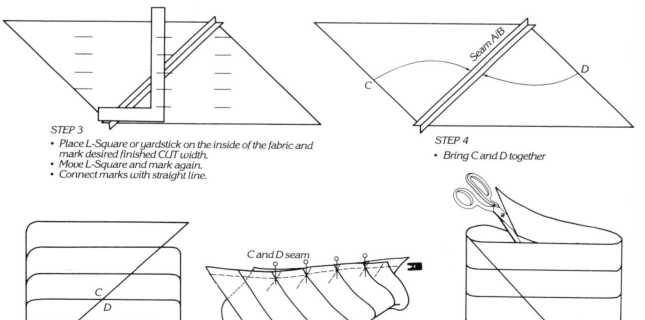

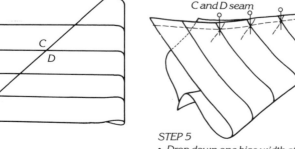

STEP 5
- *Drop down one bias width at top and bottom.*
- *Match marked lines, pin and sew C and D seam allowance together where the marked line crosses.*

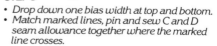

STEP 6
- *Begin cutting on the marked lines and see how easy it is to make bias.*

Binding the Vest

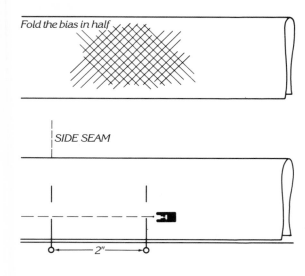

Fold the bias in half

SIDE SEAM

2"

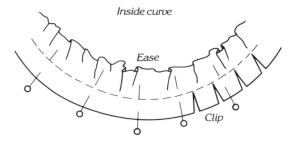

Inside curve

Ease

Clip

- Fold the 3" (7.6 cm) wide bias in half and press. (Double fold bias is stronger and looks better.)

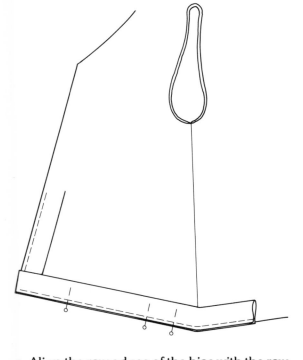

- Align the raw edges of the bias with the raw edges of the outside of the vest.
- Starting at the bottom an inch or two beyond the side seams, place a few pins ahead of you and begin sewing. Sew ½" (12 mm) in from the raw edges. Pin ahead and sew until you get to the first curve or point. Stitch slowly and carefully—now is not the time to hurry.

- If it is an outside curve, slightly ease extra fullness into the bias. A little extra fullness will help to keep the bias from cupping or pulling toward the back.
- If it is an inside curve, slightly pull on the bias so it will cup.
- If it is a point, you will make a double mitered corner.

Mitered Corners

- Sew right up to ½" (12 mm) away from the front corner. Leave the machine needle in the fabric. Cut a strip of stiff cardboard or plastic approximately ⅜" (10 mm) wide (or the width of your desired finished bias).

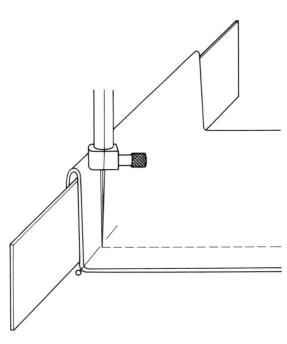

- Hold the plastic strip up, perpendicular to the fabric and at a 45" angle to the corner.
- Bring the fabric straight up and over and down the other side of the strip (just pretend it is an ant crawling over a fence).
- Place a cornerstone pin ½" (12 mm) from the edge on the other side of the strip.

25

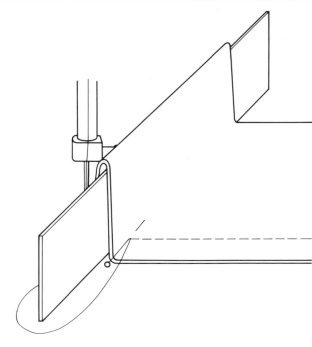

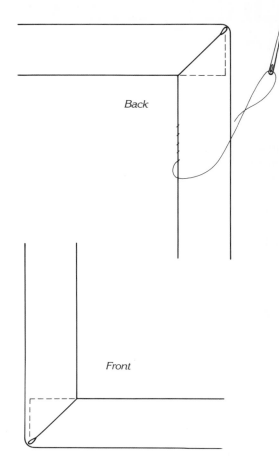

Back

Front

- Lift the presser bar and pull the fabric away from the needle, giving you about 6″ (15.3 cm) of loose threads.
- Place the machine needle into the bias on the other side exactly where you had pinned it with the cornerstone pin. Remove the cornerstone pin and continue sewing. When you get to the inside curve at the neck, pull the bias slightly so that it will cup or turn easily to the back. The smaller the curve, the more you will pull the bias.
- Sew around to where you started. Cut this end of the bias about 1″ (2.5 cm) longer than needed.
- Clip both inside and outside curves. Trim all edges as needed to a scant ¼″ (6 mm).

- Bring bias to the back and hand sew to the lining. Use a matching thread and a fine blind hem stitch. When you get to the point, tuck the miter into the opening on the front and the back, forming a double miter.
- Stitch closed and continue hemming.

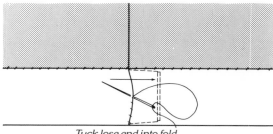

Tuck lose end into fold

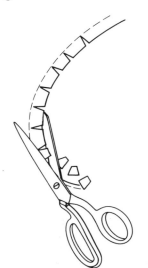

Lining the Vest
Method 3

- In this method, the vest is sewn by machine around all the outer edges except the armholes. This vest is turned through one armhole. The armholes are then sewn closed by hand. This method is used for grid vests and the rainbow panel, etc. where the side seam was eliminated in the pattern and the vest.

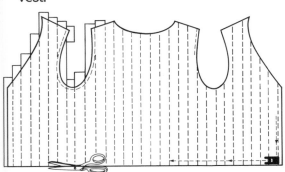

- Trim the outer vest to the original pattern size.
- Stay stitch around all edges at ¼″ (6 mm).
- Use the trimmed vest or the original pattern as a guide to cut the lining.

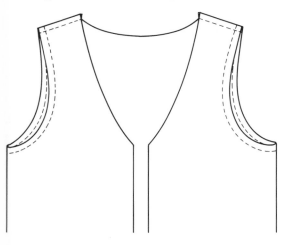

- Sew the shoulder seams together using a ½″ (12 mm) seam.
- Sew the lining shoulder seams using a ½″ (12 mm) seam.
- Open seams and press.

- Stay stitch around the lining and vest armholes. This needs to be exactly where you will be turning this seam inside, or ½″ from the edge.
- Clip curves of armholes *very* carefully to stay stitched line.

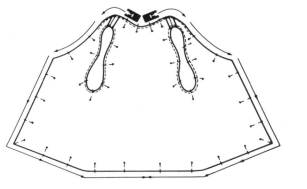

- Place the lining on the vest, right sides together. Pin around all edges.
- Machine stitch the neck edge, fronts and bottom, ½″ (12 mm) from edge, beginning at the center top. Sew to center bottom.
- Go back and begin again at center top and sew the other way around to center bottom.

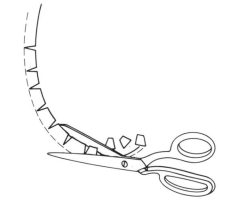

- Clip curved seams about every ½″ (12 mm).
- Trim all the outer seam allowances to about ⅛″ (3.2 mm), not the armholes.
- Turn the vest entirely through one armhole (both armholes must be open).
- Press, using a damp pressing cloth.

27

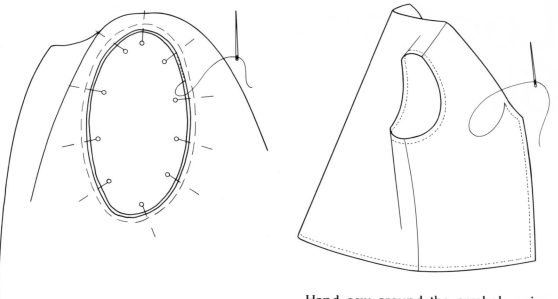

- Turn the seam allowances of the armhole to the inside. Press carefully.
- Baste around the armhole, or pin carefully.

Hand sew around the armhole using a matching thread and small, even, blind hem stitches. Top stitch with Perle cotton around all edges.
- Press as needed, and wear it!

NOTE: Use the trimmed vest or the original pattern as a guide to cut the lining.

Log Cabin, Patchwork, String and Grid Piecing

The Random Log Cabin Vest

Color plates pages 49, view 2, page 54, view 20

Materials

	CHILD 2–8	JUNIOR 5–9	ADULT	
			8–12	14–22
Fabric Center Square	¼ yd (.23 m)	¼ yd (.23 m)	¼ yd (.23 m)	¼ yd (.23 m)
6–10 coordinated	¼ yd each (.23 m)	¼ yd each (.23 m)	¼ yd each (.23 m)	⅜ yd each (.34 m)
Batting	½ yd (.46 m)	¾ yd (.68 m)	¾ yd (.68 m)	1½ yd (1.4 m)
Lining	½ yd (.46 m)	¾ yd (.68 m)	¾ yd (.68 m)	1½ yd (1.4 m)

NOTIONS:
1 large spool thread, neutral to the selection, 1½" (3.8 cm) cutting guide, scissors, marking tools, # 8 Perle cotton, #8 Crewel needle, pins, plastic, 4 buttons.

REFER TO:
1) Fabric Preparation, page 10.
2) Making & Fitting the Trial Vest, page 12.
3) Stack Cutting, page 15.
4) Log Cabin Practice Block, page 31.
5) Lining the Vest, Method 1, page 17.

This vest is the first in the book for many reasons. It was the first one made and the one from which all the others grew. It was first pieced by Margaret Ana to coordinate with my *Log Cabin Jacket*.

This vest is one of the easiest in this book. It includes many construction techniques which makes it a great stepping stone for the quilter who wants to become more involved with clothing and creativity.

If you have any sort of "textile collection" you may go directly to it, pull out six or eight coordinated fabrics and get started. You've heard about make-it-today, wear-it-tomorrow. This is one of those.

Stack cut the fabric. Refer to page 15 for general instructions for stack cutting. Cut all the strips 1½" (3.8 cm) wide from selvage to selvage. Remove the selvages. Cut all the fabric. It may be more than you will need but I am sure that after you see how easy this is you will go on and make another one for someone. DO NOT cut the center square fabric into strips. Place all of the strips into a paper bag and mix them up.

Remember, if your fabrics were coordinated to begin with they will remain so as you select randomly from the bag. This method will help you to get started and help eliminate the guesswork.

Occasionally you will pull out one strip which is the same as the last one. Just put it back in the bag and take another one.

LOG CABIN PRACTICE BLOCK

Log cabin blocks are begun in the center with a square, and strips or rows are added in a circular pattern from the center out. After piecing this vest you will realize that the strip widths may vary and the center square may be large or small, and the log cabin will usually come out alright.

You will use all 1½" (3.8 cm) wide strips for the practice block.

- Cut one 10" (25.4 cm) square of batting, (Pellon Fleece if you have it).

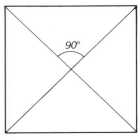

Mark diagonal guidelines through the center.

- Cut one 3" (7.6 cm) square of fabric for the center.

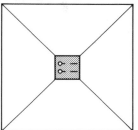

Place the center square of fabric right side up on the guidelines. Hold the center square in place with two pins.

- Take one strip of fabric from the bag.
- Place this strip right side down on top of the center square.

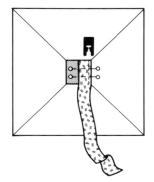

Sew from the top to the bottom through the fabric and the batting. Use a ¼" (6mm) seam (or the width of the presser foot).

Do not pre-cut the lengths of fabric, you will cut after you sew. Cut the strip even with the bottom of the center square.

Finger press and pin.

31

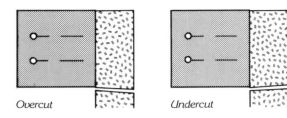

Overcut   Undercut

NOTE: *If you "undercut" the strip it will not be long enough to be caught in the next seam. In the beginning, it will be better to slightly overcut the end of the strip so that when you flip it out you will have enough fabric for a good seam allowance. You can trim the excess, if you wish, after you sew the next strip.*

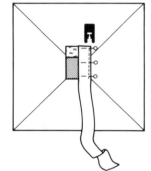

Turn the block in a counterclockwise rotation so that the last row added is at the top.

Place the next strip at the top of the last row added, right sides together. Pin and sew from the top to the bottom.

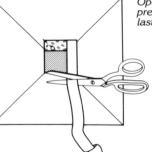

Open the strip, finger press, cut even with the last strip.

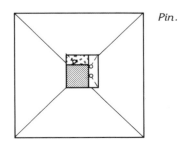

Pin.

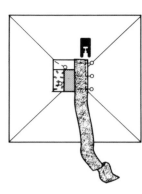

Turn the block counterclockwise again.

Take another strip from the bag. Pin and sew from top to bottom.

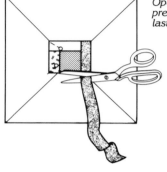

Open the strip, finger press, cut even with the last strip and pin.

- Now, if all is going well, you will see what the diagonal guidelines are for. The first row out from the center, or Log 1, will never touch the diagonal guidelines, BUT THE UPPER LEFT HAND CORNER of the next three strips WILL touch the guidelines. Do they?

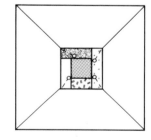

If not, observe how you are sewing. Continue sewing the logs in this rotating manner until you have sewn three rows out from the center. Now, isn't that fine? Trim the batting on the practice block to a neat square, edges even with the fabric.

- Stay stitch around all the outer edges, ½" (12 mm) from the edge. Use this practice block for the cording or bias binding lesson. You are now ready to piece your vest.

CHECK LIST:

- Is the block too large? Use more seam allowance.
- Is the block too small? Use less seam allowance.
- Are you finger pressing and pinning each strip?
- Is the center square straight?
- Turn the practice block over; it will be easy for you to see your sewing errors.
- There is no need to backstitch when you sew the strips, since each new row added secures the last.

LOG CABIN
RANDOM VEST BACK

- Mark and cut one plastic template for the center back square from the pattern, fig. A.
- Mark the center back line on the batting.
- Mark up from the hem line 7" on the center back line, or height desired according to length if adjusted.
- Place two corners of the template on the

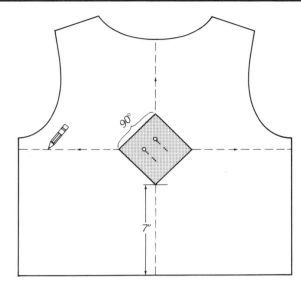

marked line. Mark around the template, mark lines to the sides.
- Cut one center back square of fabric.
- Place and pin the center back square of fabric on the marked lines.

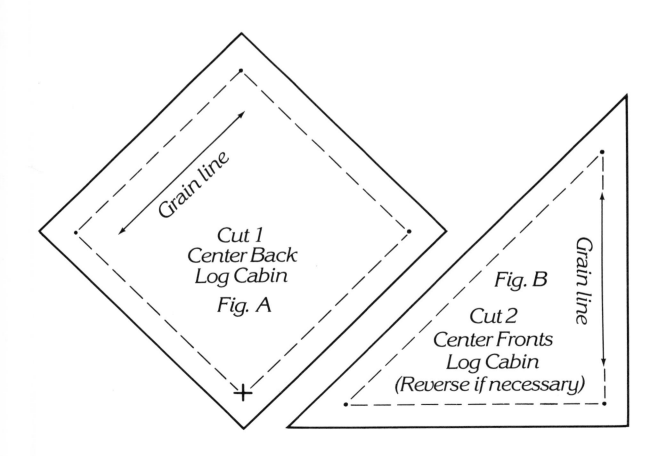

Grain line

Cut 1
Center Back
Log Cabin

Fig. A

Fig. B

Cut 2
Center Fronts
Log Cabin
(Reverse if necessary)

Grain line

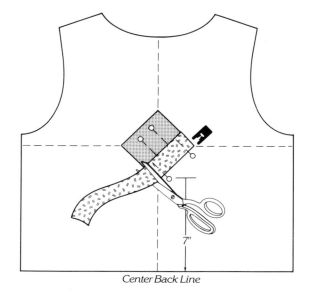

Center Back Line

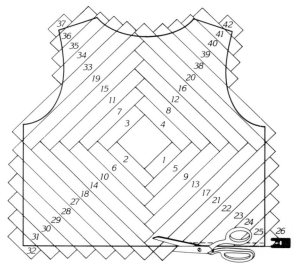

Numbers indicate sewing sequence

- Take one strip of fabric from the bag of assorted fabrics.
- Place the strip right sides together on top of the center back square.
- Pin in place.
- Sew from top to bottom ¼" (6 mm) from the edge.
- Open the strip, finger press, cut and pin.

- Continue sewing strips until you fill up the batting.
- Trim the vest back to the original pattern size.
- Stay stitch around all the edges ¼" (6 mm) from the edge.

LOG CABIN RANDOM VEST FRONTS
- Make one plastic template from the pattern given, figure B, page 33.

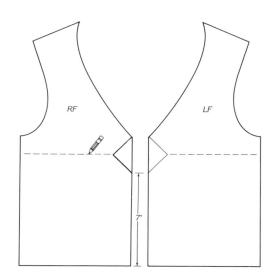

- Turn the vest counterclockwise one quarter turn.
- Add one more strip. Pin and sew from the top to the bottom.
- Open the strip, finger press and cut the strip.
- Pin the strip open.

- Cut two front half squares of fabric.
- Pin one half square of fabric to the left front 7" (17.8 cm) above the hem line on the center front.
- Mark horizontal lines from the corner of the half square to the sides.

34

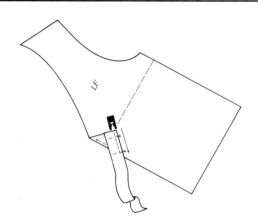

- Take one strip of fabric from the bag.
- Place this strip right side down over the center half square.
- Pin and sew from the center line to the edge.

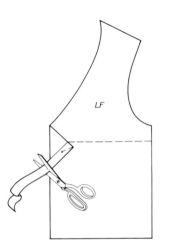

- Open this strip, finger press and cut even with the edge.

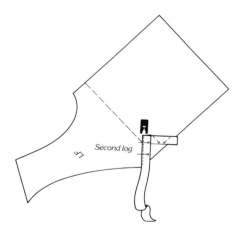

- Turn the batting vest around.
- Add another strip to the center front.
- Sew from the inside to the outside edge.

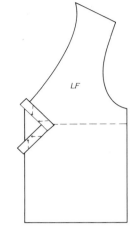

- Open the strip, finger press, trim and pin.
- Continue sewing strips to the right front in this alternating manner until the batting is filled.
- Sew the left front in the same manner.

Stay stitch ¹/₄" from edge

- Trim the fronts to the original pattern size.
- Stay stitch around all the edges ¹/₄" (6 mm) from the edge.
- Your first vest is now pieced.
- You are ready to assemble the vest.
- Please refer to: *Lining the Vest, Method 1,* page 17.

Planned Log Cabin Vest

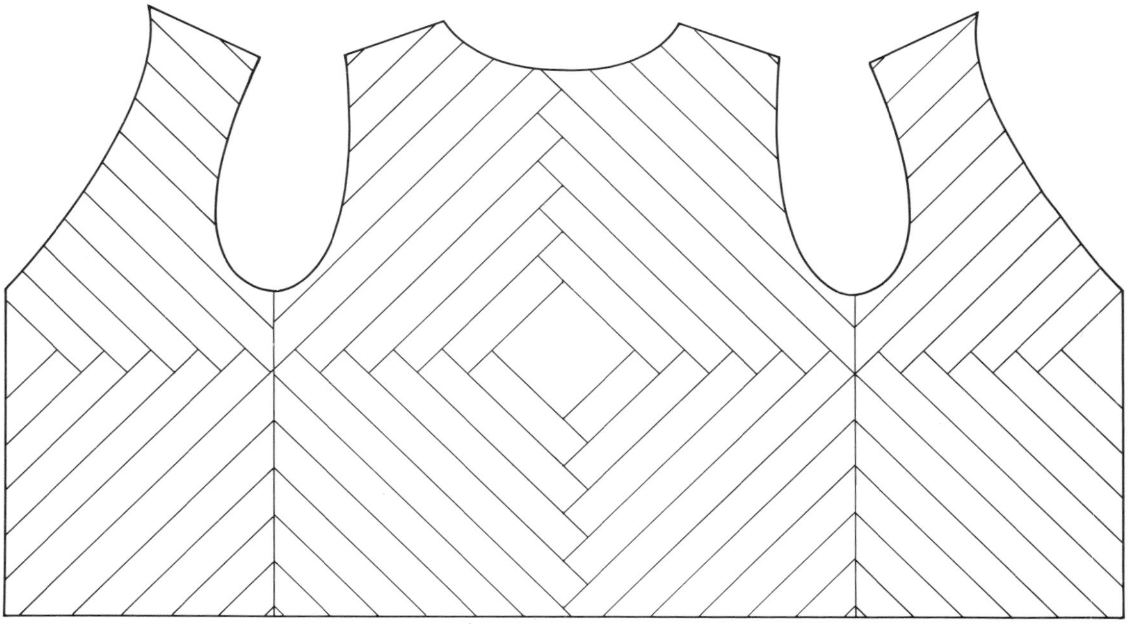

Color plates page 50 view 4, 5 page 51, view 6

Materials

	CHILDS 2–8	JUNIORS 5–9	ADULTS 8–12	14–22
Center Square	¼ yd (.23 m)	¼ yd (.23 m)	¼ yd (.23 m)	¼ yd (.23 m)
Fabric (yards)				
1 (A)	¼ yd (.23 m)	¼ yd (.23 m)	¼ yd (.23 m)	⅜ yd (.34 m)
2 (B)	¼ yd (.23 m)	¼ yd (.23 m)	¼ yd (.23 m)	⅜ yd (.34 m)
3 (C)	¼ yd (.23 m)	¼ yd (.23 m)	¼ yd (.23 m)	⅜ yd (.34 m)
4 (D)	¼ yd (.23 m)	¼ yd (.23 m)	¼ yd (.23 m)	⅜ yd (.34 m)
5 (E)	¼ yd (.23 m)	¼ yd (.23 m)	¼ yd (.23 m)	⅜ yd (.34 m)
6 (F)	¼ yd (.23 m)	¼ yd (.23 m)	¼ yd (.23 m)	⅜ yd (.34 m)
7 (G)	¼ yd (.23 m)	¼ yd (.23 m)	¼ yd (.23 m)	⅜ yd (.34 m)
8 (H)	¼ yd (.23 m)	¼ yd (.23 m)	¼ yd (.23 m)	⅜ yd (.34 m)
9 (I)	¼ yd (.23 m)	¼ yd (.23 m)	¼ yd (.23 m)	⅜ yd (.34 m)
10 (J)	¼ yd (.23 m)	¼ yd (.23 m)	¼ yd (.23 m)	⅜ yd (.34 m)
11 (K)	¼ yd (.23 m)	¼ yd (.23 m)	¼ yd (.23 m)	⅜ yd (.34 m)
12 (L)	¼ yd (.23 m)	¼ yd (.23 m)	¼ yd (.23 m)	⅜ yd (.34 m)
Batting	½ yd (45.7 cm)	¾ (.7 m)	¾ (.7 m)	1½ (1.4 m)
Lining	½ yd (45.7 cm)	¾ (.7 m)	¾ (.7 m)	1½ (1.4 m)

NOTIONS: Thread, 1 large spool neutral to the total selection, scissors, 1½″ (3.8 cm) cutting guide, plastic, marking tools, #8 Perle cotton, #8 Crewel needle, 4 buttons.

REFER TO:
1) Fabric Preparation, page 10.
2) Making & Fitting the Trial Vest, page 12.
3) Stack Cutting, page 15.
4) Log Cabin Practice Block, page 31.
5) Lining the Vest, Method 1, page 17.

This vest uses the Log Cabin technique to create an all-over, planned look. Twelve solid fabrics are used—four sets of colors with three values (light, medium, and dark) in each color. The range of colors may be very close, giving an all-over, muted look, or you may wish to use white, grey, and black for a more striking look. Pastels create a lovely spring look. Whatever you choose, the look will be created by your fabric choice. Finding the right fabrics for this vest may take more time than for most of the other vests. It is difficult for most shops to carry such a wide range of solids. Do persist in working on the fabric selection for this vest. It will be worth all your effort.

PIECING THE BACK

- Cut one plastic template from fig. A, page 33.
- Mark a center back line on the batting.
- Measure up 7" (17.8 cm).
- Place the bottom corner of the template 7" (17.8 cm) up from the bottom.
- Mark around the template.
- Draw lines from the template to the sides.
- Cut one center back square of fabric, using the plastic template.
- Pin the center square, right side up on the center square on the back.

PLANNED LOG CABIN
Tape fabric to diagram.

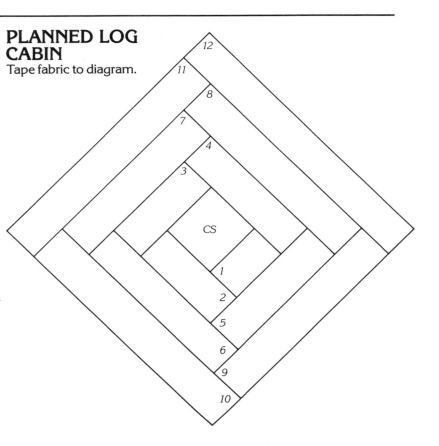

- Refer to your planned arrangement for the fabric placement.
- Refer to: *Stack Cutting,* page 15. Stack cut the fabric.
- Sew the back as you did for the practice block, page 31. And the *Random Log Cabin* back, page 33.

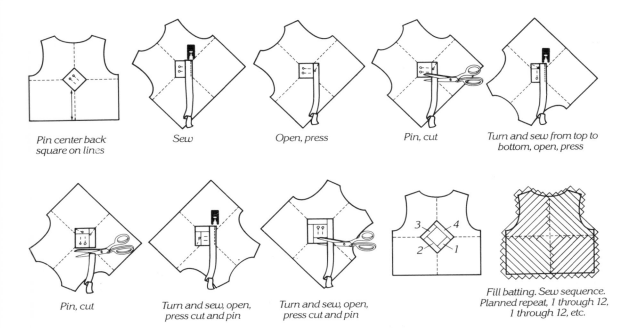

Pin center back square on lines

Sew

Open, press

Pin, cut

Turn and sew from top to bottom, open, press

Pin, cut

Turn and sew, open, press cut and pin

Turn and sew, open, press cut and pin

Fill batting. Sew sequence. Planned repeat, 1 through 12, 1 through 12, etc.

PIECE THE FRONTS

- Cut one template, from the pattern given for the center front half squares, fig. B, page 33.
- Measure up 7″ (17.8 cm) from the bottom.
- Place the half square template on this mark and mark around the template.
- Mark lines to the sides from the corner of the half square. Repeat for the other side.

- Pin the finished back up in front of you for reference. Piece the fronts following the plan of the back. Refer to: *Practice Block*, page 31.
- Sew the fronts.

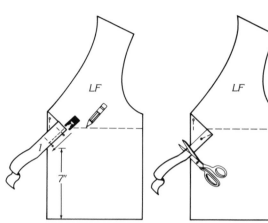

Place front triangle 7″ above bottom edge. Mark horizontal line to side. Follow planned sequence. Place row 1 right side to triangle. Sew from top to edge.

Open, press, cut and pin.

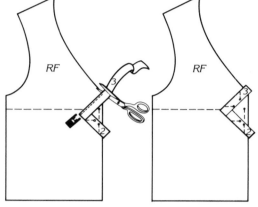

Follow planned arrangement. Sew row 2 to right front. Open, press and pin. Sew row 3 to right front.

Open, cut and pin.

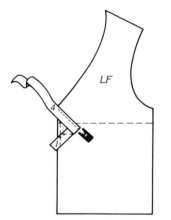

Sew row 4

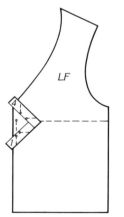

Open, cut and pin.

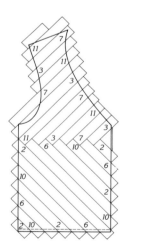

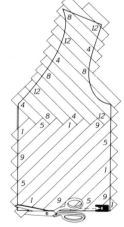

Continue sewing the rows following the planned sequence.

- Trim to the original pattern size.
- Stay stitch around all edges ¼″ (6 mm) from edge. You are now ready to line your vest.
- Refer to: *Lining the Vest, Method 1*, page 17.

Dutchman's Puzzle
(Center Block in the back)

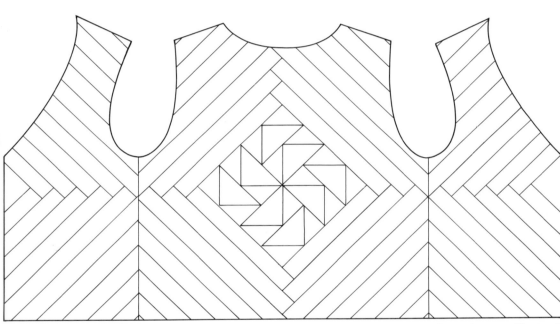

Color plate page 51, view 8

Materials

	CHILD 2–8	JUNIOR 5–9	ADULT 8–14	ADULT 16–22
Fabric: 8 to 10	¼ yd (.23 m) each	¼ yd (.23 m) each	¼ yd (.23 m) each	½ yd (.46 m) each
Batting	½ yd (.46 m)	¾ yd (.68 m)	¾ yd (.68 m)	1½ yds (1.4 m)
Lining	½ yd (.46 m)	¾ yd (.68 m)	¾ yd (.68 m)	1½ yds (1.4 m)

NOTIONS: Thread; #8 Perle cotton; #8 Crewel needle; 1½″ (3.8 cm) cutting guide; scissors; marking tool; buttons (optional); plastic sheet, 8″ x 10″ (20.3 x 25.4 cm).

REFER TO:
1) Fabric Preparation, page 10.
2) Making and Fitting the Trial Vest, page 12.
3) Stack Cutting, page 15.
4) Log Cabin Practice Block, page 31.
5) Lining the Vest, Method 1, page 17.

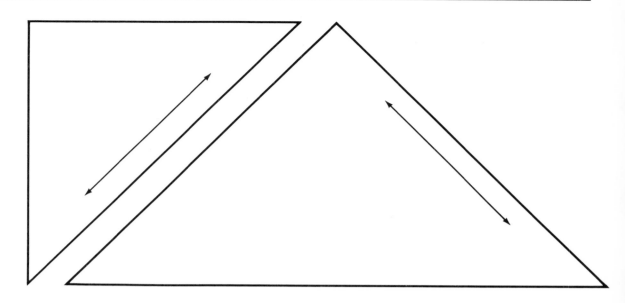

DUTCHMAN'S PUZZLE

Almost any 8″ (20.3 cm) to 12″ (30 cm) block can be used for the center design. Designs which look good when set on point are best. There are over 300 suitable patterns—do investigate! Haven't you made up a block and never used it? Well, now is the time to dig it out. Thirty accurate 12″ (30 cm) blocks can be found in my *Sampler* book.

Margaret Ana used the Dutchman's Puzzle on page 38 of *The Sampler Quilt.*

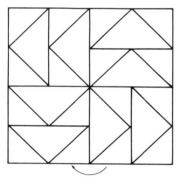

Step 4 Sew the two halves together. Press and trim.

Step 1 Sew two small triangles to one large triangle. Sew the remaining 7 units together. Press the seams up.

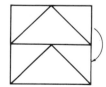

Step 2 Sew two small units together forming one block of the four patch. Sew the remaining small units together.

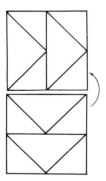

Step 3 Sew two halves of the block together. Sew the other half together.

THE BACK

• Position the block on the center of the batting. Pin in place.

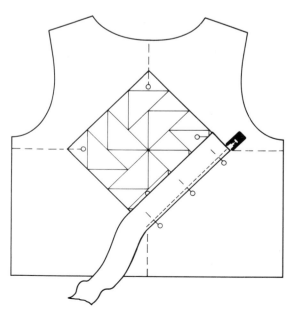

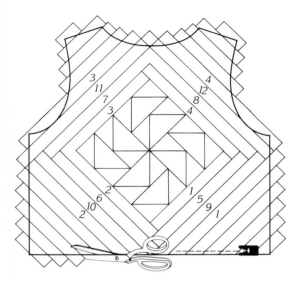

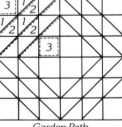

- Fill the back of the vest with strips. Strips cut 1½" wide following the *Practice Block,* page 31 and *Log Cabin Vest Back,* page 33.
- Trim the vest back to the original pattern size.

- Trim the vest fronts to the original pattern size.
- Stay stitch around all edges ¼" from edge. Refer to: *Lining the Vest, Method 1,* page 17.

VEST FRONTS

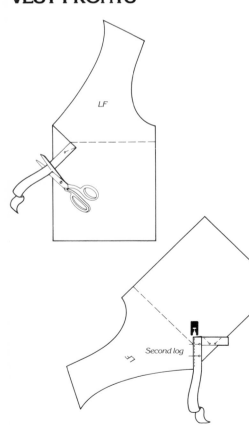

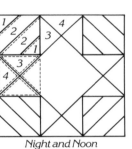

Jinx Star

Night and Noon

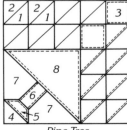

Flying Geese

Garden Path

- Fill the batting following the Random Log Cabin method, page 34.

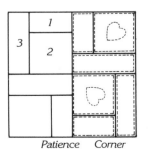

Patience Corner

Pine Tree

Pastel Fan Vest

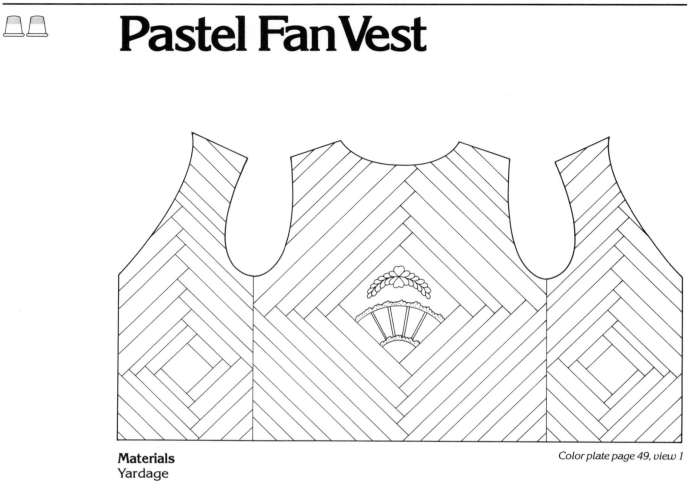

Materials
Yardage

Color plate page 49, view 1

	CHILDS 2–8	JUNIORS 5–9	ADULTS 8–14	ADULTS 16–22
Fabric 8 different	¼ yd (.23 m) each	¼ yd (.23 m) each	¼ yd (.23 m) each	⅜ yd (.34 m) each
Lace &/or trim of 8 different	½ yd (.46 m) each	½ yd (.46 m) each	1 yd (.91 m) each	1 yd (.91 m) each
Ribbon ⅛" (3.2 mm)	3 yd (2.7 m)	4 yd (3.6 m)	5 yd (4.57 m)	5 yd (4.57 m)
Lining	½ yd (.46 m)	¾ yd (.7 m)	¾ yd (.7 m)	1½ yd (1.4 m)
Batting	½ yd (.46 m)	¾ yd (.7 m)	¾ yd (.7 m)	1½ yd (1.4 m)
Hankies*	5	5	5	5

NOTIONS: Scissors; embroidery floss; large spool neutral thread.
REFER TO:
1) Fabric Preparation, page 10.
2) Making and Fitting the Trial Vest, page 12.
3) Stack Cutting.
NOTE: *The strip width varies. Cut two strips 1" (2.5 cm), cut two strips 1¼" (3.2 m), cut the rest 1½" (3.8 cm).*
4) Random Log Cabin Vest, page 31.
5) Handquilting, page 78.
6) Lining the Vest, Method 2, page 22.

Read following instructions before buying the hankies.

Sonia Bertsch has created a pair of vests for mother and daughter. The matching vests are soft and feminine, and a great project for grandma.

The center back motif was made of five embroidered hankies that were cut up to piece the fan. Strings or strips of fabric and lace were used to fill out the surrounding batting in the quilt-as-you-sew technique. Touches of embroidery were added after the fronts and backs were pieced.

Cut 1 plastic template

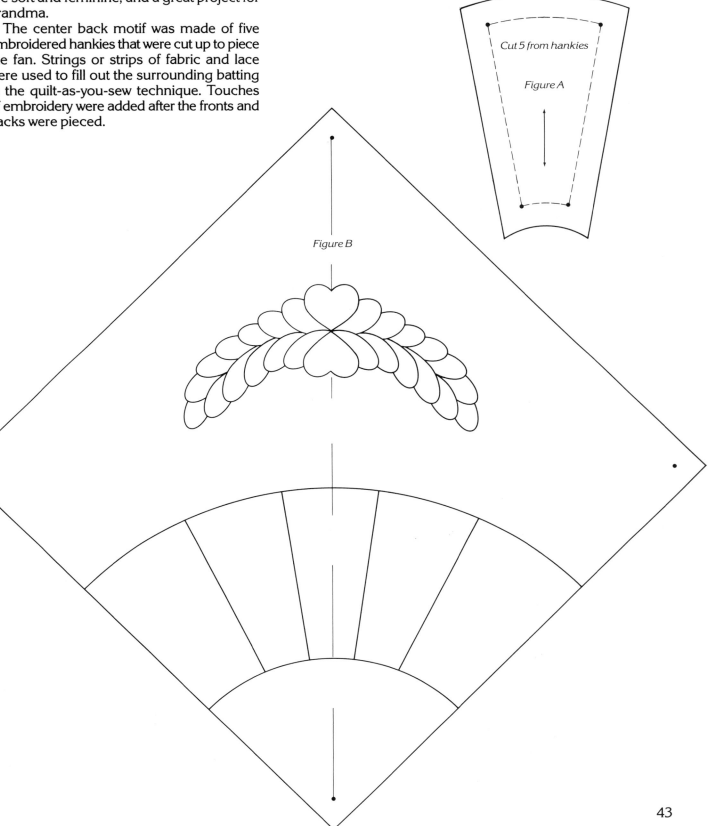

Cut 5 from hankies

Figure A

Figure B

PIECING THE FAN

- Cut one plastic template for the fan, fig. A. *NOTE: Take this template to the store with you to use for placement when selecting your hankies. You may be able to save and get two or three designs from one hankie.*
- Place the template over the embroidered designs on the hankie. Mark around template. You will need five fan pieces.
- Cut fan pieces from hankie(s) and sew together, using ¼" (6 mm) seam.

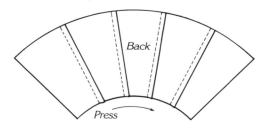

- Press the seams in one direction.
- Trim seams to ⅛" (3.2 mm)
- Cut a 5½" (13 cm) square of solid fabric for the center block in the back of the vest, fig. B.
- Fold in half on the diagonal and finger press.
- Place fabric over the square in the book, page 43.
- Trace the quilting lines and the placement lines for appliqueing the fan.

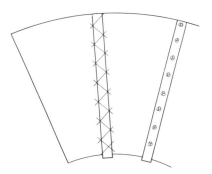

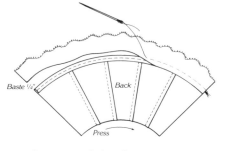

- Baste the top of the fan seam allowance under ¼" (6 mm).
- Baste a narrow, ruffled eyelet to the back of the fan at the top.

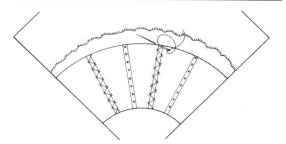

- Baste the pieced fan to the placement lines in the square.
- Use a fine blind hem stitch to applique fan to the square.
- Turn under bottom of fan and sew to block. Clip as needed.

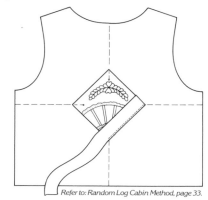

Refer to: *Random Log Cabin Method, page 33.*

- Center appliqued square on the center of the batting back.
- Pin and/or baste the center square to the batting.

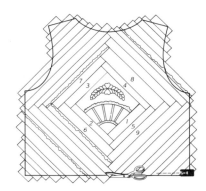

- The vest back is finished by sewing strips to fill up the batting as in the *Random Log Cabin,* page 31.
- While you are sewing the random strips, lace and trims, pin the trims into the seam. Many of the trims and ribbons may be added after the vest is pieced.
- Trim the edges and staystitch ¼" (6 mm) from edge around vest back.

FRONTS

- Make one plastic template for front center.
- Cut two center front squares from hankies.
- Draw center line on batting fronts.
- Position plastic template on batting front line as shown, 3" (7.6 cm) from the hemline.
- Mark around the template.
- Mark guidelines to sides from the corners of vest.

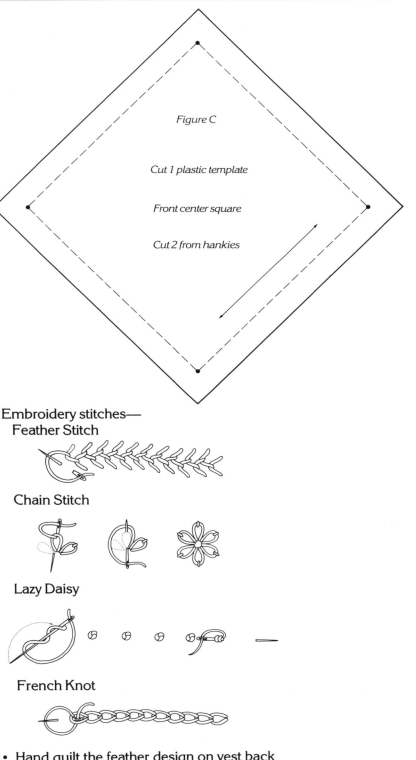

Figure C

Cut 1 plastic template

Front center square

Cut 2 from hankies

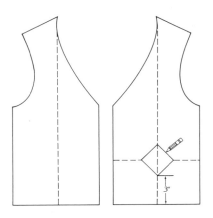

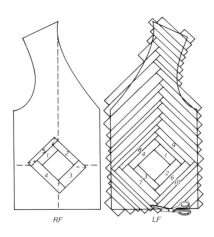

RF   LF

- Pin center hankie squares to marked lines.
- The fronts need to be mirrored:
  Following the diagram, begin on either side of the top of the front square. The fabrics are not exactly mirrored—just the sewing sequence. The strips should continue to be used at random.
- Remember to add lace trims as you sew the random strips.
- The vest fronts are finished using the *Random Log Cabin technique,* page 34.
- Add decorative touches to finished vest.

Embroidery stitches—
Feather Stitch

Chain Stitch

Lazy Daisy

French Knot

- Hand quilt the feather design on vest back block. Refer to: *Hand Quilting,* page 78.
- Add bows of ribbons to the vest center squares by hand. Ribbons may be used on the front for closures.
- Trim the vest to the original pattern.
- Stay stitch ¼" (6 mm) from all edges. Refer to: *Lining the Vest, Method 2,* page 22.

45

Denim Log Cabin

Color plate page 51, view 6

Materials

	CHILD 2–8	JUNIOR 5–9	ADULT 8–14	ADULT 16–22
Fabric	¾ yd (.68 m)	1 yd (91.4 cm)	1¼ yd (1.14 m)	1½ yd (1.4 m)
Denim Bias	½ yd (.46 m)	½ yd (.46 m)	¾ yd (.7 m)	¾ yd (.7 m)
Center Square	¼ yd (.23 m)	¼ yd (.23 m)	¼ yd (.23 m)	¼ yd (.23 m)
Batting	½ yd (.46 m)	¾ yd (.7 m)	¾ yd (.7 m)	1½ yd (1.4 m)
Lining	½ yd (.46 m)	¾ yd (.7 m)	¾ yd (.7 m)	1½ yd (1.4 m)
Tear Away Stabilizer	½ yd (.46 m)			

NOTIONS: Thread (1 large spool), fabric glue stick, machine embroidery thread, open-toe foot, 1½" (3.8 cm) cutting guide, scissors.

CHILD'S VEST—REFER TO:
1) Stack cutting, page 15.
2) Machine Applique Practice Block, page 90.
3) Log Cabin Practice Block, page 31.
4) Lining the Vest, Method 2, page 22.

ADULT VEST—REFER TO:
1) Making and Fitting the Trial Vest, page 12.
2) Stack cutting, page 15.
3) Log Cabin Practice Block, page 31.
4) Lining the Vest, Method 1, page 17.

ADULT LOG CABIN VEST

Jenny Gardella made her vest to go with her two-year-old grandson Matthew's vest. Since these two are so easy and cute together, I put them on the same page.

The child's vest is made in the same manner as the adult's. It just has a cute machine-appliqued center back square. The design for the snail is one of Ellen Mosbarger's. I recommend all of her books for design sources.

This vest design is very versatile. You can make it in any size, use any size center square and any design in the center square.

A photograph of the adult's Denim Vest is shown on page 51.

CHILD'S LOG CABIN VEST

The child's vests are pieced using the Log Cabin technique in that there is a center back square and strips of fabric are added to fill the batting from the center out. Sonia used silk-screened motifs for the centers. Jenny machine appliqued hers. Use the format given here and create your own child's vest.
- Cut batting to size
- Cut 1 back center square.
- Cut fabric strips 1½" (3.8 cm) wide.

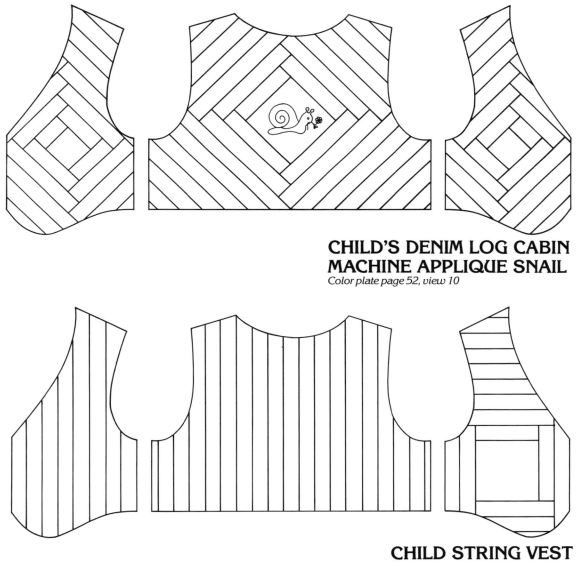

CHILD'S DENIM LOG CABIN MACHINE APPLIQUE SNAIL
Color plate page 52, view 10

CHILD STRING VEST
Color plate page 52, view 13

The child's vest ideas given here are basic formats for you to follow or expand upon. Sonia used a silk screened heart for the center of one and a silkscreened picture for the center back of the other. You may embellish in any way.

Back—CHILD'S VEST fig. 102

- Preparing back for Applique.
  Cut 1 light brown Snail's Shell, fig. 2.
  Cut 1 light blue Snail's Body, fig. a.
- Place fabric over diagram; mark lines.
- Applique the Snail, Refer to: *Machine Applique Practice Block,* page 90.
- Center block on back.
- Log cabin the vest back.
  Refer to: *Log Cabin Practice Block,* page 31.

Fronts

- Mark center lines on fronts.
- Piece fronts using Log Cabin Method, page 34.
- Reverse fronts.
- Refer to: Lining the Vest, Method 2, page 22.

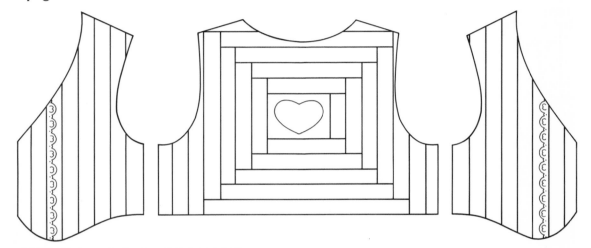

CHILD'S LOG CABIN VEST
Color plate page 52, view 12

CHILD'S RANDOM STRING VEST WITH LACE
Color plate page 52, view 11
Use this format, refer to Random Log Cabin page 30.

49

View 3.
Grid Piecing
Mountain Lake
Designed and
Pieced by
Ann West

View 4.
Planned Log Cabin
Designed by
Diana Leone
Pieced by
Margaret Ana

View 5.
Planned Log Cabin
Designed by
Diana Leone
Pieced by
Margaret Ana

50

View 6.
Planned Log Cabin
Designed and
Pieced by
Jenny Cardella

View 7.
Strip Piecing
Western Vest
Designed and
Pieced by
Ann West

View 8.
Planned Log Cabin
*Dutchman's
    Puzzle*
Designed by
Diana Leone
Pieced by
Margaret Ana

View 9.
Random Log Cabin
Nine-Patch Log
Designed by
Diana Leone

Children's Vests
Log Cabin and
 Strip
View 10 Machine
 Applique
View 11 Random
 Log Cabin
View 12 Strip
 Piecing
View 13 Strip
 Piecing
Designed and
 Pieced by
 Sonia Bertsch

View 14.
Patchwork
Rainbow Geese
Designed by
Diana Leone
Pieced by
Doris Olds

View 15.
Grid Piecing
Poppy
Designed and
Pieced by
Sondra Rudey

15

View 16.
Grid Piecing
*Trip Around
the World*
Designed by
Diana Leone
Pieced by
Ann West

16

View 17.
Sashiko
Shamrocks
Designed and
Pieced by
Sondra Rudey

View 18.
Sashiko
Wine Glass
Designed and
Pieced by
Sondra Rudey

View 19.
Sashiko
Pampas Grass
Designed and
Quilted by
Sondra Rudey

View 20.
Random Log Cabin
Designed and
Pieced by
Sondra Rudey

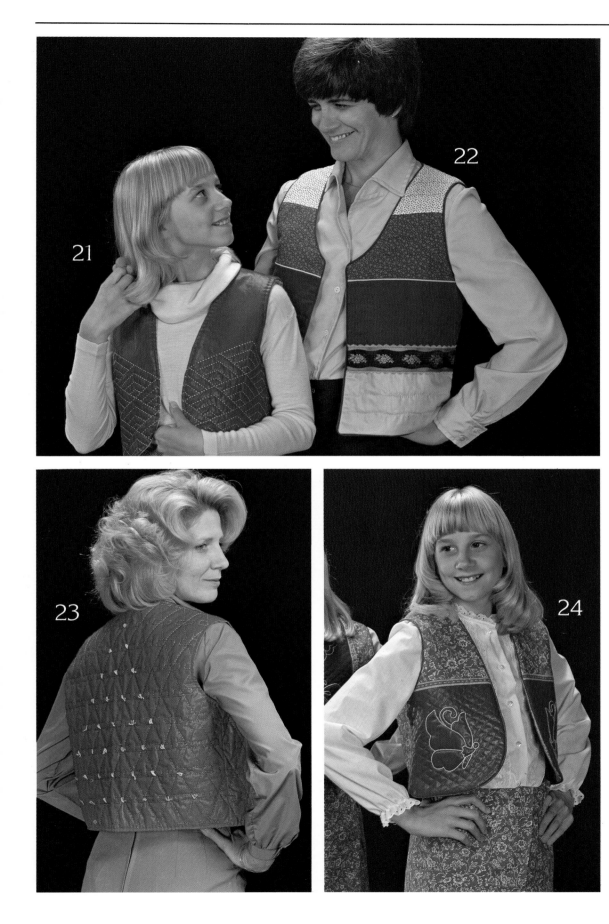

View 21.
Sashiko
Pointed Blue Ocean Waves
Designed and Quilted by Sondra Rudey

View 22.
Machine Quilting *Bertie's Ribbons*
Designed and Pieced by Bertie Booth

View 23.
Sashiko
Christmas Trees
Designed and Quilted by Ann West

View 24.
Sashiko
Purple Butterflies
Designed and Pieced by Sondra Rudey

View 25.
Machine Applique
Lotus Blossom
Designed by
Diana Leone
Pieced by
Jenny Gardella

View 26.
Machine Applique
Art Nouveau
Designed and
Pieced by
Eunice Roberts

View 27.
Machine Quilting
Bertie's Rainbow
Designed and
Quilted by
Bertie Booth

Rainbow Geese

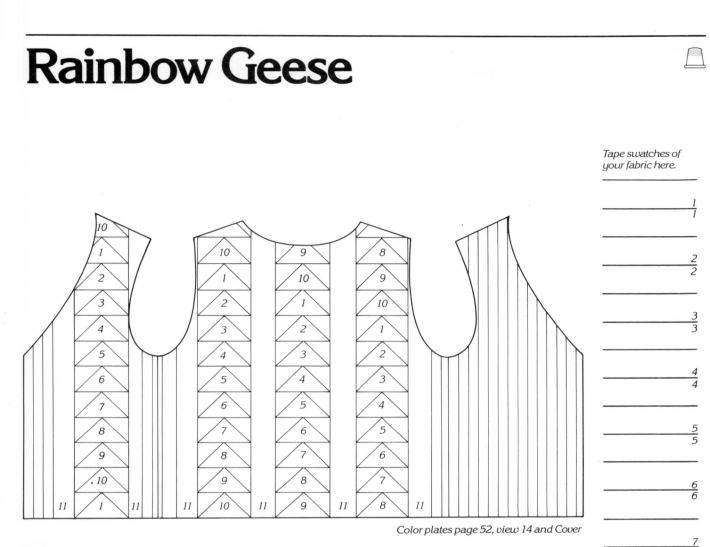

Color plates page 52, view 14 and Cover

Materials

	CHILD 2–8	JUNIOR 5–9	ADULT 8–14	ADULT 16–22
10 Solids each #1 through 10	¼ yd (.23 m)	¼ yd (.23 m)	⅜ yd (.34 m)	⅜ yd (.34 m)
10 Prints each #1 through 10	¼ yd (.23 m)	¼ yd (.23 m)	⅜ yd (.34 m)	⅜ yd (.34 m)
Striped Fabric (**) #11	½ yd (.46 m)	¾ yd (.68 m)	1 yd (.91 m)	1½ yd (1.4 m)
Solid Fabric #12 (not for Geese)	¾ yd (.7 m)	⅞ yd (.8 m)	1 yd (.91 m)	1½ yd (1.4 m)
Lining	½ yd (.46 m)	¾ yd (.7 m)	¾ yd (.7 m)	1½ yd (1.4 m)
Batting	½ yd (.46 m)	¾ yd (.7 m)	¾ yd (.7 m)	1½ yd (1.4 m)

NOTIONS: Thread—1 spool to match; 1 Size 8 Perle Cotton. Size 8 Crewel needle. Four buttons (optional). Plastic for template. Cutting guide 1½″ (3.8 cm). Scissors. Marking tools.

REFER TO:
1) Fabric Preparation, page 10.
2) Making and Fitting the Trial Vest, page 12.
3) Stack Cutting, page 15.
4) Lining the Vest, Method 1, page 17.

(**) If you use a striped fabric to make some strips, you will need seven lengths of stripe, approximately ¾ yard long each.

RAINBOW GEESE

This striking and relatively easy vest was inspired by a quilt I designed recently (Rainbow Geese #2, front cover of Quiltmakers 1983 calendar). My friend, Doris Olds, made both the quilt and the vest.

I chose solid chintz and micro dots in primary colors for the geese. The vertical strips were 2" (5 cm) wide stripes which were cut from a multiple-striped fabric. This vest could easily be made from scraps of subtle fabric from your textile collection to give a muted, antique look.

PREPARATION
- Pre-shrink all fabric. Do not shrink batting.
- Make plastic templates from actual size patterns given.

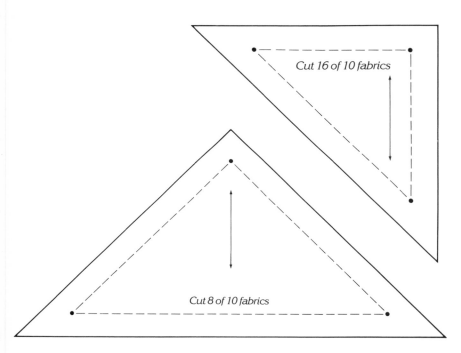

Cut 16 of 10 fabrics

Cut 8 of 10 fabrics

- Cut 8 large triangles from each of the 10 solid fabrics for the geese.
  Cut 16 small triangles from each of the 10 print fabrics for the geese.
- Stack cut 25 strips of the solid fabric #12. See *Stack Cutting,* page 15.
- Cut 6 strips from fabric #11 (striped) 27" (.7 m) long. (This will include the ¼" (6 mm) seam allowance. They may be a little wider or narrower and still be alright.

PIECING THE GEESE
- Make each unit by sewing two small triangles to one large triangle, as shown. The ¼" (6 mm) seam allowance is included.

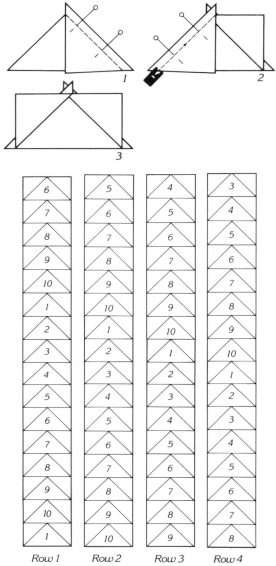

Row 1   Row 2   Row 3   Row 4

- Press all seams up.
- Sew four strips of geese (three for the back and one for the front).
- Row 1—Begin with color 1 at the bottom of the first row.
- Row 2—Begin with color 10 at the bottom of the second row.
- Row 3—Begin with color 9 at the bottom of the third row.
- Row 4—Begin with color 8 at the bottom of the fourth row.
- Sew 16 (approximately) units in each row.
- Press all seams up
- Trim seam allowances.

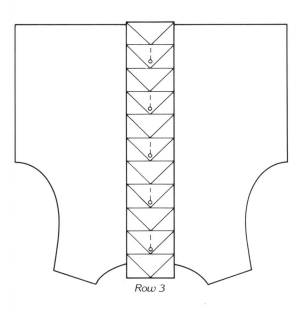

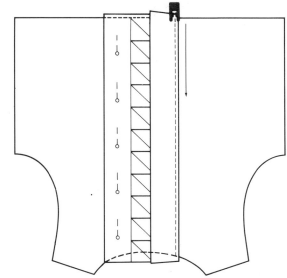

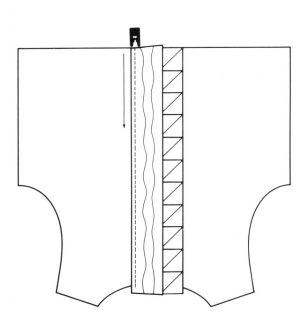

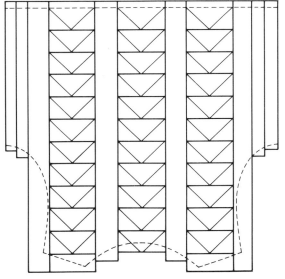

Row 3

- Pin row 3 of pieced geese to center of batting back, right side up.

- Open strip and press. Pin to hold in place.
- Sew length of striped fabric to the other side.
- Position from bottom up and pin row 2 of the pieced geese, right side down, over the striped fabric.
- Sew from bottom to top.
- Add another row of striped fabric.
- Repeat for other side of back.

- Pin a length of the striped fabric, right side down, on top of the right hand edge of the center row of geese.
- Sew from bottom to top (use a dual-feed foot if possible). Always sew from bottom to top, so that the geese will remain aligned at bottom edge.

- Using the solid fabric #12 (which you have cut in 1½" (3.8 cm) strips) fill up the rest of the batting back in the quilt-as-you-sew technique.
- Reposition pattern on finished back to check for final size. Mark around pattern and trim all edges.
- Stay stitch around all edges ¼" (6 mm) from edge.

59

Fronts

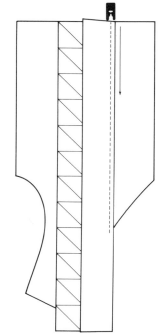

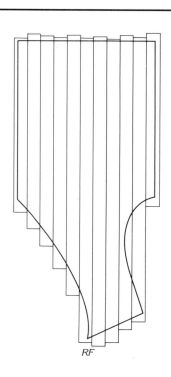

RF

- Positioning from bottom up, center Row 4 on right vest front, right side up, and pin in place. Place a length of the striped fabric, right side down, on top of the right hand edge of Row 4. Sew from bottom to top.
- Place another length of the striped fabric on other side of Row 4. Sew from bottom to top.

- The left front vest is stripped with the solid fabric. Start at center front, following placement line, and work out to side edge. Sew from bottom to top.
- Press with warm iron and damp pressing cloth.
- Reposition pattern on finished fronts. Mark around pattern and trim all edges.
- Stay stitch ¼" (6 mm) from all edges.
- Refer to: *Lining the Vest, Method 1,* page 17.

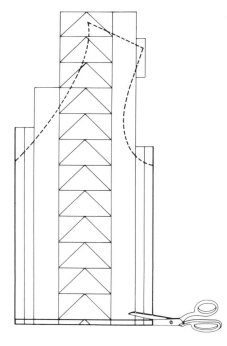

- Fill up the rest of the right vest front with the other solid fabric, as you did for the back.

Grid Piecing

The design possibilities for grid piecing are limitless. Any design from a landscape to a simple object may be translated into squares with the use of graph paper and colored pencils. Accuracy in piecing is imperative, but with a little practice, you will enjoy this creative process. Our grid patchwork was inspired by Cheryl Grieder Bradkin when she taught the method in my shop.

GRID PRACTICE BLOCK

I highly recommend that you take a moment or two and make this practice block. In doing so you will go through the entire process and realize how easy it really is.

		C		
	C		C	
C		A		C
	A	B	A	
C	A	B	A	B	A	C
	A	B	A	
C		A		C
	C		C	
		C		

PREPARATION

- Cut one strip of fabric #A 1½″ (3.8 cm) by 18″ (45 cm).
- Cut one strip of fabric #B 1½″ (3.8 cm) by 18″ (45 cm).
- Cut two strips of fabric #C 1½″ (3.8 cm) by 43″ (107.5 cm).
- All fabrics will be cut 1½″ (3.8 cm) wide from selvage to selvage. Remove the selvages. The grain line will go up and down. The fabric is marked on the wrong side (if you can tell). The fabric is placed wrong side up on the table (or flannel board for the full vest).
- The sewing machine must be close to your laid out fabrics. Sew all seams with ¼″ (6 mm) seam.

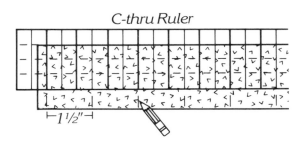

C-thru Ruler

- Place fabric #A right side down on a flat surface. Use the C-Thru ruler and mark 9 lines 1½″ (3.8 cm) apart. Cut the fabric apart on the marked lines.

Materials—Grid pieced practice block.

Fabric
¼ yd (.23 m) color A
¼ yd (.23 m) color B
¼ yd (.23 m) color C

NOTIONS: Three pencils to match fabric, C-Thru ruler (B-85), 1½″ (3.8 cm) cutting guide, scissors, thread to match, ¼ yd (.23 m) Pellon Fleece® or similar lightweight batting, walking foot, single needle throat plate, single needle foot.

- Place these 1½″ (3.8 cm) cut squares, wrong side up, on a flat surface in the order they appear in the diagram, fig. a, page 61. You will need four 1″ (2.5 cm) squares of fabric B. Cut these and lay these out according to your diagram.
- You will need two 1½″ (3.8 cm) squares of fabric #C for the Center Row. Mark, cut and lay these out, according to the diagram.
- For rows 1 and 4 you will need four strips of fabric #C 2½″ (6.4 cm) long. For rows 2 and 5 you will need four strips of fabric #C 3½″ (8.9 cm) long. For rows 3 and 6 you will need two strips of fabric #C 7½″ (19 cm) long. Mark, cut and lay these pieces out.
- All fabrics should be placed right side down so that when you pick up the pieces you can pin and take them directly to the sewing machine.
- Place the single needle throat plate and single needle foot on your machine.
- Shorten your stitch length to 12–14 stitches per inch (6 stitches per cm). Sew the pieces into strips.

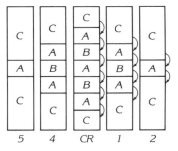

5	4	CR	1	2
C	C	C	C	C
	C	A	C	C
	A	B	A	
A	B	A	B	A
	A	B	A	
C	C	A	C	C
		C		

- Sew the Center Row first.
- Sew C to A to B to A to B to A to C.

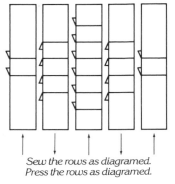

Sew the rows as diagramed.
Press the rows as diagramed.

- Press CR seams up.
- Seams will be pressed in alternating directions; i.e., center row, all seams up; rows 1 and 4 press seams down; rows 2 and 5 press seams up. Continue pressing in same manner.
- Cut one 7½″ square of thin batting.

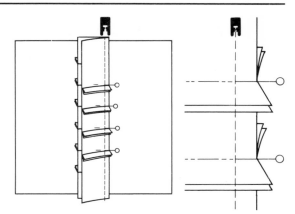

Where the pin goes in at the seam allowance will be your sewing guideline.

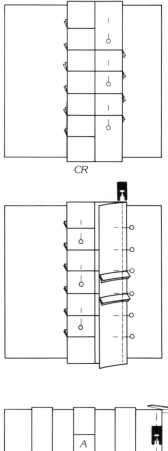

CR

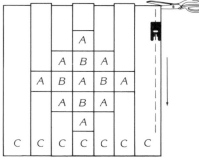

Mountain Lake

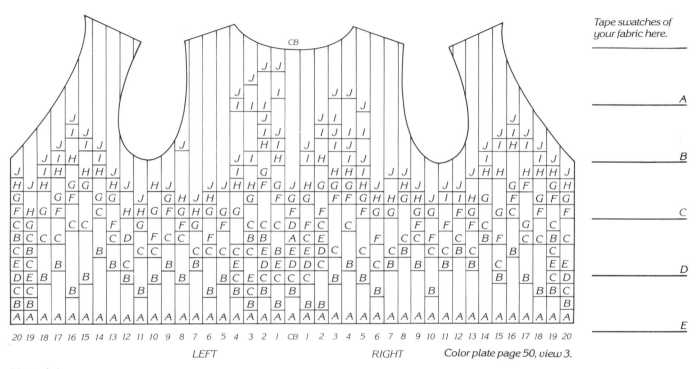

20 19 18 17 16 15 14 13 12 11 10 9 8 7 6 5 4 3 2 1 CB 1 2 3 4 5 6 7 8 9 10 11 12 13 14 15 16 17 18 19 20

LEFT   RIGHT   *Color plate page 50, view 3.*

Materials

	CHILDS 2–8	JUNIORS 5–9	ADULTS 8–12	ADULTS 14–22
J Sky Blue	¼ yd (.23 m)	½ yd (.46 m)	½ yd (.46 m)	⅝ yd (.57 m)
I White	¼ yd (.23 m)	¼ yd (.23 m)	¼ yd (.23 m)	¼ yd (.23 m)
H Dark Brown	¼ yd (.23 m)	¼ yd (.23 m)	¼ yd (.23 m)	¼ yd (.23 m)
G Medium Brown	¼ yd (.23 m)	¼ yd (.23 m)	¼ yd (.23 m)	¼ yd (.23 m)
F Light Brown	¼ yd (.23 m)	¼ yd (.23 m)	¼ yd (.23 m)	¼ yd (.23 m)
E Dark Lake Blue	¼ yd (.23 m)	¼ yd (.23 m)	¼ yd (.23 m)	¼ yd (.23 m)
D Medium Lake Blue	¼ yd (.23 m)	¼ yd (.23 m)	¼ yd (.23 m)	¼ yd (.23 m)
C Dark Green	¼ yd (.23 m)	¼ yd (.23 m)	⅜ yd (.34 m)	⅜ yd (.34 m)
B Medium Green	¼ yd (.23 m)	¼ yd (.23 m)	⅜ yd (.34 m)	⅜ yd (.34 m)
A Grass Green	¼ yd (.23 m)	⅜ yd (.34 m)	⅜ yd (.34 m)	½ yd (.46 m)
Batting (thin)	½ yd (.46 m)	¾ yd (.7 m)	¾ yd (.7 m)	1½ yd (1.4 m)
Lining	½ yd (.46 m)	¾ yd (.7 m)	¾ yd (.7 m)	1½ yd (1.4 m)

NOTIONS: Thread, one large spool (neutral color); pattern paper, 1 yd.; 1½″ (3.8 cm) cutting guide; scissors; ¼″ (6 mm) graph paper (4 per inch); colored pencils to match 10 fabrics; #8 Perle cotton; #8 Crewel needle; C-Thru ruler, B-85.

REFER TO:
1) Fabric Preparation, page 10.
2) Making and Fitting the Trial Vest, page 12.
3) Stack Cutting, page 15.
4) Grid Piecing Practice Block, page 61.
5) Lining the Vest, Method 3, page 27.

Ann designed this vest, which looks much more complicated than it really is. The original drawing was done on ¼" (6 mm) grid paper. Each ¼" (6 mm) square = 1" (2.5 cm) finished. She traced her size pattern, overlapped the side seam allowances, and cut the batting for the entire vest. The small pieces of fabric for the scene were cut and sewn together in vertical strips. These pieced strips were then sewn to the batting in the "quilt-as-you-sew" method, beginning in the center back. The batting was filled with the pieced strips. The outer edges were trimmed and basted. The vest was lined using Method 3, and hand stitched around the edges.

MAKING THE ONE PIECE PATTERN

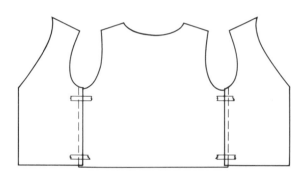

- Make practice block, Grid Piecing, page 61.
- Trace your size onto pattern paper.
- Eliminate the side seam on the pattern.
- Overlap the pattern pieces at the side seam ½" (12 mm).
- Tape the seams together.
- Pin the pattern to the batting.
- Mark around the pattern. Cut out the batting 1" (2.5 cm) larger than the pattern.

NOTE: The diagram is for a size 12. To adjust add or delete under the arm holes and fronts. The finished strips are 1" wide. Measure your pattern and count how many you will need.

PIECING THE VEST

- Cut strips of each fabric 1½" (3.8 cm) wide, from selvage to selvage. Trim off selvages. You will need only two strips each of the white (I) and light brown (F); one strip of medium lake blue (D); one strip dark lake blue (E).
- Cut the rest of the fabric into strips 1½" wide.
- Separate the strips and place them in front of you.

- Follow the diagram and begin with the center back strip (CR). A count (of the chart) will show you that you need 3 inches (7.6 cm) of grass green (A) plus the seam allowance (¼ + ¼ = ½) = 3½" (6 mm + 6 mm = 12 mm) = 8.8 cm.
- Take a strip of grass green (A) and mark 3½" (8.8 cm) (this will include the ¼" (6 mm) seam for the top and the bottom of the strip.
- Cut the 3½" (8.8 cm) of grass green (A) and place it on a flat working surface, close to your sewing area.
- Count the next graphed color, which will be a 1" square (2.5 cm²). Cut a 1½" (3.8 cm) piece of the medium green (B). Continue counting, cutting, and laying out your pieces until you have all the rows cut.

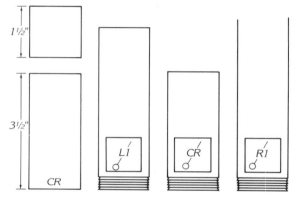

- Stack the pieces by row and label with a numbered paper pinned to the stack.

SEWING THE STRIPS

- Use a neutral thread, not white.
- Sew all seams using ¼" (6 mm) seam.
- Use a single needle throat plate and a single needle foot.
- Shorten the stitch length to 12 to 14 stitches per inch (6 per cm).

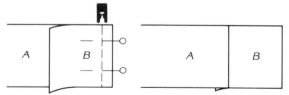

The pin goes in at exactly ¼" (6 mm) from the edge.

- Begin with the center row (CR).
- Pin the bottom grass green (A) piece to the second medium green (B) piece.
- The pins properly placed will be your sewing guide.
- Sew these pieces together. Remove the pins as you sew to them.

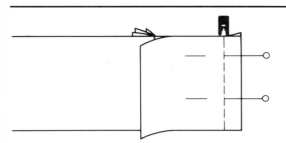

- Open, finger press (seams toward bottom).
- Take the next piece (which should be dark green C) from the center row stack. Pin and sew.
- Continue sewing pieces in this manner until all the vertical strips are sewn. Yes, it takes some time, but it is worth it!
- Layout all of your sewn strips in order wrong side up.
- Press the rows in alternating directions.

SEWING THE STRIPS TO THE BATTING

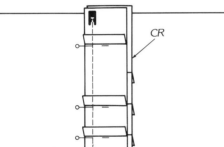

- Place and pin the center row (CR), right side up, on the center back of the batting.
- Align the bottom of the strip with the marked line at the bottom.

- Pin right strip 1, right sides together with CR.
- Pin each butted seam exactly ¼" (6 mm) from the edge.
- Sew from the bottom to the top, slowly and carefully.
- Remove pins as you come to them.
  (If at all possible use the walking foot for all the quilt-as-you-sew process).
- Press and pin.
- Continue sewing the vertical strips until all of the batting is filled.
- Your outer vest is now pieced.
- Press, using a damp pressing cloth.
- Place the original pattern on the vest and mark carefully around the pattern, aligning the hem line.
- Trim the vest to the original pattern. Staystitch ¼" (6 mm) from all edges. Staystitch ½" (12 mm) from armhole edge. Use your trimmed vest for the pattern to cut the lining.
- Cut out your lining. Staystitch ½" (12 mm) from edges of armholes. Refer to: *Lining the Vest, Method 3*, page 27.

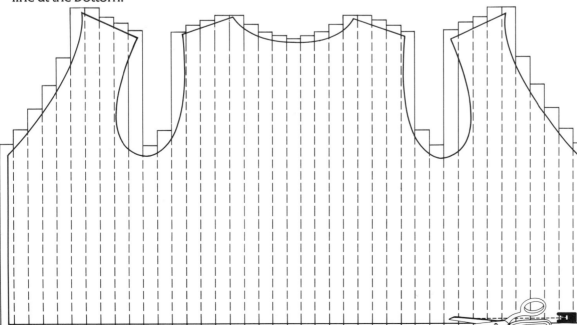

Trip Around the World

Tape swatches of your fabric here.

_____ A

_____ B

_____ C

_____ D

_____ E

_____ F

_____ G

_____ L

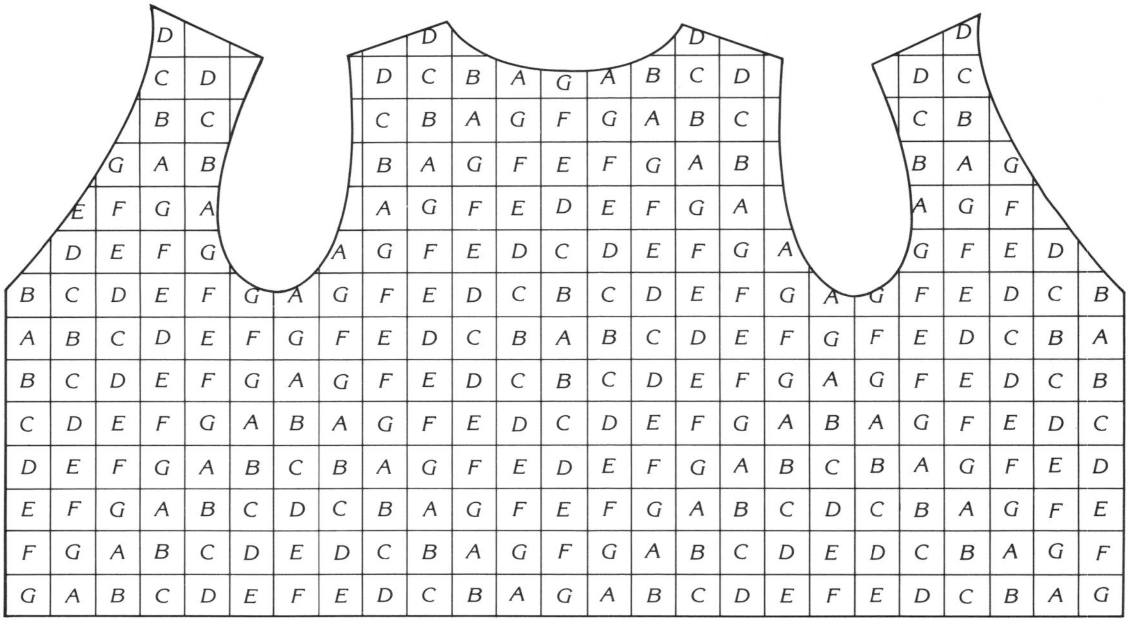

Color plate page 53, view 16

Materials

Fabric	CHILDS 2–10	JUNIOR 5–9	ADULT 8–14	ADULT 16–22
A	¼ yd (.23 m)	¼ yd (.23 m)	⅜ yd (.34 m)	⅜ yd (.34 m)
B	¼ yd (.23 m)	¼ yd (.23 m)	⅜ yd (.34 m)	⅜ yd (.34 m)
C	¼ yd (.23 m)	¼ yd (.23 m)	⅜ yd (.34 m)	⅜ yd (.34 m)
D	¼ yd (.23 m)	¼ yd (.23 m)	⅜ yd (.34 m)	⅜ yd (.34 m)
E	¼ yd (.23 m)	¼ yd (.23 m)	⅜ yd (.34 m)	⅜ yd (.34 m)
F	¼ yd (.23 m)	¼ yd (.23 m)	⅜ yd (.34 m)	⅜ yd (.34 m)
G	¼ yd (.23 m)	¼ yd (.23 m)	⅜ yd (.34 m)	⅜ yd (.34 m)
Lining	½ yd (.46 m)	¾ yd (.7 m)	¾ yd (.7 m)	1½ yd (1.4 m)
Batting	½ yd (.46 m)	¾ yd (.7 m)	¾ yd (.7 m)	1½ yd (1.4 m)

NOTIONS: 1 Large spool of neutral thread, not white; #8 Perle cotton; #8 Crewel needle; scissors; 2¼" cutting guide; colored pencils to match fabric; plastic for templates; C-Thru ruler B-85; 1½ yards (1.4 m) flannel for wall; single needle throat plate; single needle foot; walking foot (dual feed foot).

REFER TO:
1) Fabric Preparation, page 10.
2) Making and Fitting the Trial Vest, page 12.
3) Stack Cutting, page 15.
4) Grid Piecing Practice Block, page 61.
5) Lining the Vest, Method 1, page 17.

I had originally planned on showing you how to use Helen and Blanche Young's efficient piecing method for the *Trip Around the World.* After a month of rewording their book, I decided to use the grid method. If you want to try their method, by all means do. You'll love it and probably make a quilt to match.

VEST BACK

- All strips will be cut 2¼" (5.6 cm) wide, selvage to selvage. Remove selvages after cutting.
- Cut the strips into 2¼" (5.6 cm) squares.
- Stack the squares in order.
- Place the stacks in a row close to the sewing machine.

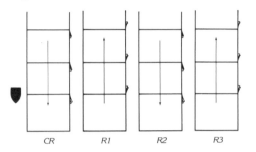

CR   R1   R2   R3

- Piece Center Row (CR). 1 square = 1¾" (4.4 cm) finished.
- Beginning at the bottom, sew the first fabric to the second, right sides together, until the row is pieced.
- Press all seams toward the bottom.
- Place the pieced strip (row) back in order.
- Piece all the rows, following your design.
- Press in alternating directions, i.e., right row 1 up; right row 2 down, etc.

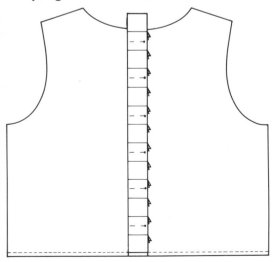

- Pin the Center Row (CR) on the center of the batting back.
- Align the bottom square with the hemline.

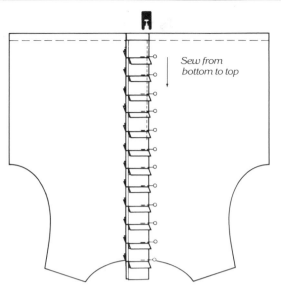

Sew from bottom to top

- Pin the left row #1 on top of CR, right sides together. Pin carefully.

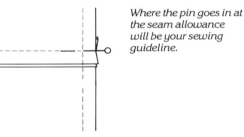

Where the pin goes in at the seam allowance will be your sewing guideline.

- Sew from bottom to top. Use a walking foot if possible.
- Open, press and pin.

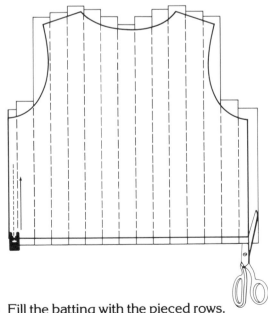

- Fill the batting with the pieced rows.
- Trim to original pattern.
- Stay stitch ¼" from edges.

67

VEST FRONTS
- You will have two Center Rows (CR).

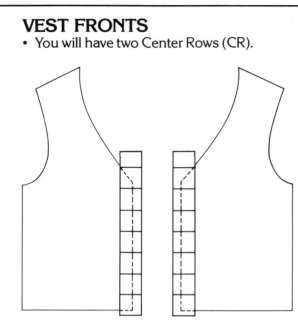

G	F	E	D	C	B	A
F	E	D	C	B	A	G
E	D	C	B	A	G	F
D	C	B	A	G	F	E
C	B	A	G	F	E	D
B	A	G	F	E	D	C
A	G	F	E	D	C	B
G	F	E	D	C	B	A
A	G	F	E	D	C	B
B	A	G	F	E	D	C
C	B	A	G	F	E	D
D	C	B	A	G	F	E
E	D	C	B	A	G	F
F	E	D	C	B	A	G

A	B	C	D	E	F	G
G	A	B	C	D	E	F
F	G	A	B	C	D	E
E	F	G	A	B	C	D
D	E	F	G	A	B	C
C	D	E	F	G	A	B
B	C	D	E	F	G	A
A	B	C	D	E	F	G
B	C	D	E	F	G	A
C	D	E	F	G	A	B
D	E	F	G	A	B	C
E	F	G	A	B	C	D
F	G	A	B	C	D	E
G	A	B	C	D	E	F

- You will position the pieced center rows on the batting, carefully aligning these rows so that they will match.

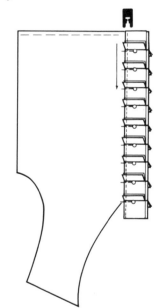

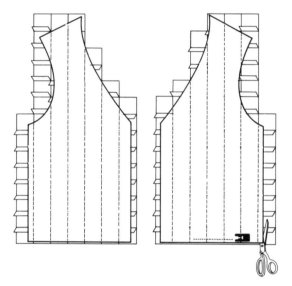

- Trim the fronts to the original pattern size.
- Staystitch ¼″ (6 mm) from the edge.
- Use the trimmed vest parts for the pattern to cut the lining.
  Refer to: *Lining The Vest Method 1,* page 17.

- Sew from bottom to top.
- Sew rows to batting until filled.

Poppy

Color plate page 53, view 15

Materials

Fabric	CHILD 2–8	JUNIOR 5–9	ADULT 8–12	ADULT 14–22
A (Rust)	⅛ yd (.11 m)	⅛ yd (.11 m)	⅛ yd (.11 m)	⅛ yd (.11 m)
B (Orange)	⅛ yd (.11 m)	⅛ yd (.11 m)	⅛ yd (.11 m)	⅛ yd (.11 m)
C (Peach)	⅛ yd (.11 m)	⅛ yd (.11 m)	⅛ yd (.11 m)	⅛ yd (.11 m)
D (Green)	¼ yd (.23 m)	¼ yd (.23 m)	¼ yd (.23 m)	¼ yd (.23 m)
E (Blue)	1 yd (.91 m)	1½ yds (1.4 m)	2 yds (1.8 m)	2½ yds (2.2 m)
Lining	½ yd (.46 m)	¾ yd (.7 m)	¾ yd (.7 m)	1½ yds (1.4 m)
Bias	½ yd (.46 m)	½ yd (.46 m)	¾ yd (.7 m)	¾ yd (.7 m)
Cording	2 yds (1.8 m)	2 yds (1.8 m)	3 yds (2.7 m)	3 yds (2.7 m)

NOTIONS: Thread, 1½" (3.8 cm) cutting guide, scissors, marking tools, colored pencils to match fabric, cording foot, zipper foot.

Refer to:
1) Fabric Preparation, page 10.
2) Making and Fitting the Trial Vest, page 12.
3) Stack Cutting, page 15.
4) Grid Piecing Practice Block, page 61.
5) Lining the Vest, Method 1 and Method 1A, page 17.
6) Continuous Bias for Binding, page 23.

Sondra Rudey designed this easy grid design of the California Poppy for the back of her vest. Cheryl Grider Bradkin gave Sondra the pattern in her Seminole workshop. The free form poppy design was machine embroidered to the fronts. This was a first for Sondra. If she can do it so can you.

PIECING THE VEST

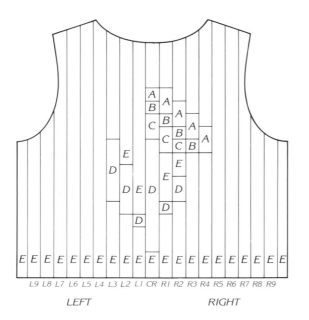

LEFT   RIGHT

- Cut out the fabrics according to the diagram.
- Cut 18-1½″ by 45″ (3.8 cm x 115 cm) strips of light blue fabric E for adult sizes. (Refer to: *Stack Cutting,* page 15.)
- Cut 2 strips, green fabric D, cut 1 strip peach fabric C, 1 orange fabric B, 1 rust fabric A.

Piecing the Back
- Piece poppy as diagrammed.
- Sew the cut pieces together into rows.
- Sew rows to the batting, beginning with the Center Row (CR). Use a short stitch on the machine, 12 to 14 stitches per inch (6 per cm). Pin carefully. Where the pin goes in will be your sewing guide. Sew the rows to the batting from the bottom to the top. Remove the pins as you sew to them.
- Use a walking foot if possible.
- Open the row, press, and pin in place. Continue adding rows, pinning carefully, until the batting is filled. Refer to: *Grid Piecing Practice Block,* page 61.
- Trim the vest to the original pattern size.
- Staystitch around all the edges, ¼″ (6 mm) from the edges.

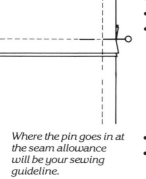

Where the pin goes in at the seam allowance will be your sewing guideline.

MACHINE EMBROIDERY

Free machine embroidery means that you are in total control of the movement of the fabric under the needle. You are drawing a picture or following a line with the threaded needle.

While careful work requires some practice, I think that free machine work is great for the beginner who is not inhibited. This process is also great for the young sewer.

I did my first piece of free machine embroidery over ten years ago. I had no idea what I was doing, I just drew some figures on the cloth, removed the foot on the machine, lowered the feed dog, and sewed merrily on. That wall piece won Best-of-Show at a major museum and entitled me to a one-woman show which literally launched my career.

In 1975 I was home on Labor Day and decided that I would machine quilt a quilt for my son.

The quilt was well basted and I had drawn feather wreathes around all the borders.

Again, I just took the foot off the machine, lowered the feed dog and hand guided the fabric under the quickly paced needle. The job was finished in one day, and it looked good. I am proud of that work, but to this day it has not been shown because I do not feel that machine quilting has yet come into its own.

It will, though, and the Janie Warnicks and other creative machine stitchers of this world will come into their own. If you want to have a little fun and see your results quickly, try a little free machine embroidery or "hand guided quilting."

MACHINE EMBROIDERY PRACTICE BLOCK

- Cut two 12″ squares (30 cm²) of any light-weight fabric.
- Cut one 12″ square (30 cm²) of medium or lightweight batting. Draw some circles, or trace the *Poppy design,* page 71.
- Baste the two layers together, well, every three inches (7.6 cm) or so, in both directions.
  Use a contrast thread on the machine.
  Do not use the free arm, you need the machine in a bed.
- Remove the foot from the machine.
- Read Darning in your manual.
- Lower the feed dog. Your hands become the hoop to hold the fabric and add a little tension.

- Bring the bobbin thread up, hold the two threads when you begin.
- Lower the needle into the fabric and begin.
- Move your hand in a circular fashion guiding the fabric under the needle following your drawn lines.

Now for the free advice. It will be easier if the needle goes fast and the hands go slow. You will see that if the needle goes slow and so do the hands you will get skips in your stitches. Try for a smooth and steady movement of the hands and a smooth but fast movement of the needle. Sew the longest continuous line you can without cutting the thread. Since you've done so well on the quilted practice block you are ready to machine embroider or "quilt" your vest.

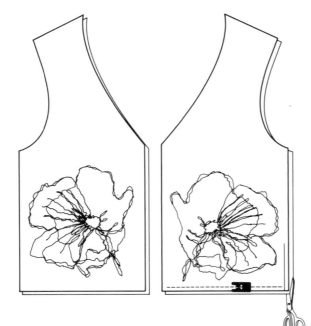

Fronts—Machine Embroidery

- Place the outer vest fabric over the poppy design, page 71.
- Trace the poppy onto the fabric, mark lightly.
- Reverse the pattern for the other front by drawing the design onto a sheet of paper, turn the paper over and remark the design on the other side. It will be reversed.
- Baste the batting to the vest fronts.
- Machine Embroider on your vest fronts.
- Trim and stay stitch ¼" from edge.
- Refer to: *Lining the Vest, Method 1* and *1A*, page 17.

Western Vest

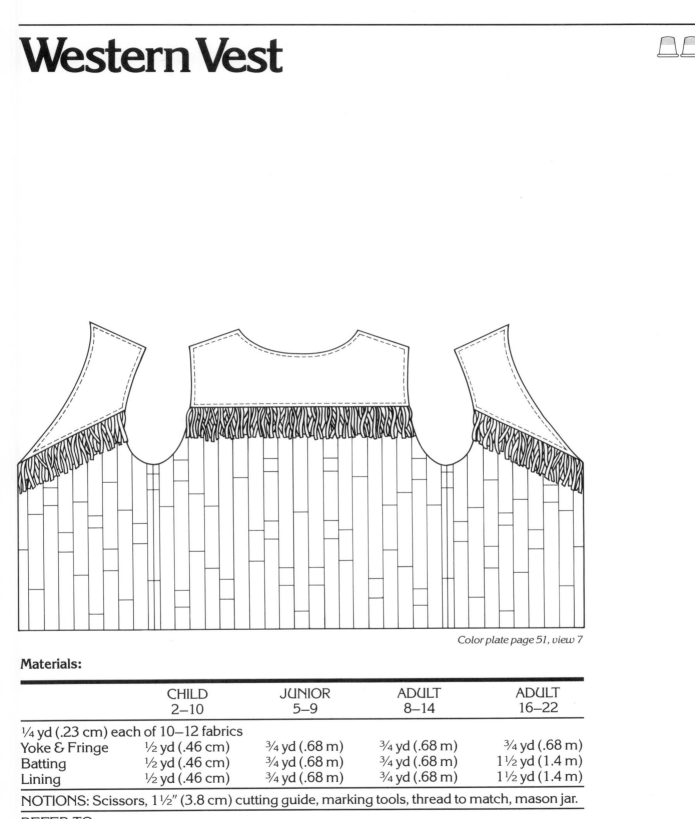

Color plate page 51, view 7

Materials:

	CHILD 2–10	JUNIOR 5–9	ADULT 8–14	ADULT 16–22
¼ yd (.23 cm) each of 10–12 fabrics				
Yoke & Fringe	½ yd (.46 cm)	¾ yd (.68 m)	¾ yd (.68 m)	¾ yd (.68 m)
Batting	½ yd (.46 cm)	¾ yd (.68 m)	¾ yd (.68 m)	1½ yd (1.4 m)
Lining	½ yd (.46 cm)	¾ yd (.68 m)	¾ yd (.68 m)	1½ yd (1.4 m)

NOTIONS: Scissors, 1½" (3.8 cm) cutting guide, marking tools, thread to match, mason jar.

REFER TO:
1) Fabric Preparation, page 10.
2) Making and Fitting the trial vest, page 12.
3) Stack Cutting, page 15.
4) Lining The Vest, Method 1, page 17.

WESTERN VEST

This western vest was styled by Ann, our tall Texan. She used twenty-eight coordinated red and blue scraps of fabrics left over from a few of her formidable projects.

The strips were pieced using little pieces of fabric to make the longer strips. These pieced strips were sewn to the batting beginning in the center of the batting and adding the pieced rows in what we call the "quilt-as-you-sew" technique. The fringe was made by cutting a strip of the denim every one fourth inch. Ann then placed it in a mason jar that was half full of water and shook it. She squeezed it and placed it in the dryer. I know that this sounds a little weird but it worked.

PIECING THE STRIPS

- Cut batting for back and fronts.

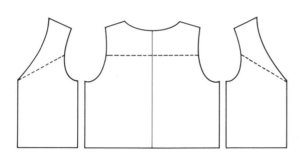

- Draw yoke placement lines on fronts as indicated on pattern.
- Stack cut the random assortment of fabric into 1½" (3.8 cm) wide strips.
- Cut these fabrics into random lengths.
- Sew these fabrics together to form long strips. Press in alternating directions, i.e. Row 1 up, Row 2 down, Row 3 up, etc.
- Sew enough strips of pieces together to fill the batting.
- As you sew pieces to make the rows lay the row on the batting. Sew twice as many as you think you will need. (The seams take up a lot of fabric.)

Back

- Sew the pieced strips to the batting in the quilt-as-you-sew technique.
- Begin in the center.
- Place the first strip right side up on the batting. Pin it in place.
- Place the first row out from the center right sides together over the center row. Pin in place.

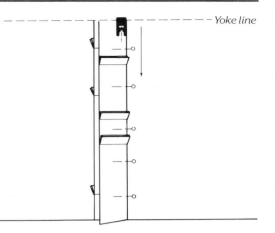

Yoke line

- Sew from the bottom of the vest to the yoke line using ¼" (6 mm) seam allowance.
- Continue sewing pieced strips to the back from the center out until you have filled the batting.

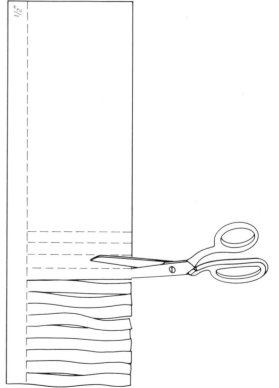

- To make fringe use a 45" (1.15 m) width of fabric by 3" (7.6 cm). Mark a line ½" (12 mm) from one long edge. Mark ¼" (6 mm) lines on the 3" (7.6 mm) direction. Cut carefully every ¼" (6 mm) to the ½" (12 mm) line.
- Place fringe in mason jar half filled with water. Shake, squeeze, and dry.

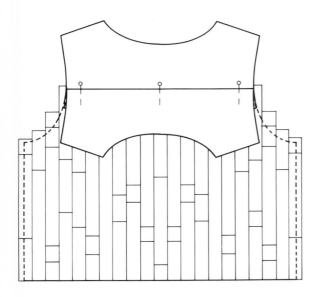

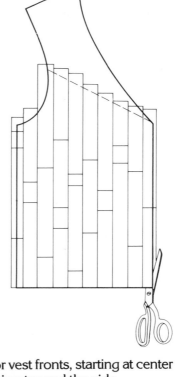

- Pin the fringe to the pieced front and back at the yoke line.
- Stay stitch in place.
- Place the yoke piece over the fringe and sew.

- Repeat for vest fronts, starting at center front and working toward the side.

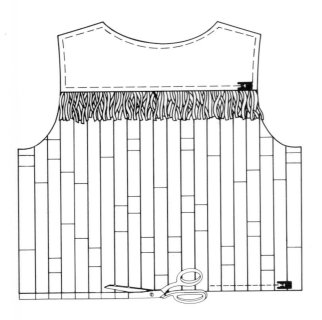

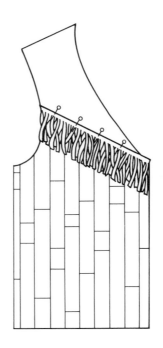

- Flip the yoke piece up and press.
- Pin in place. Top stitch around yoke.

- Pin the fringe to the front at the yoke line.

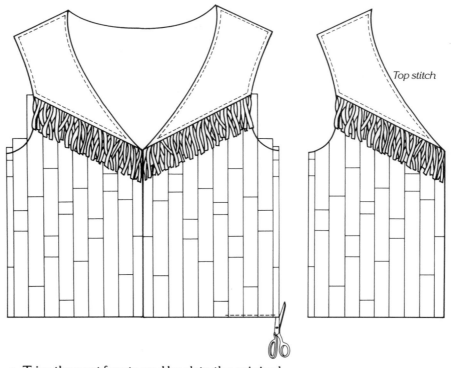

Top stitch

- Trim the vest fronts and back to the original pattern size.
- Stay stitch around all edges ¼″ (6 mm) from the edges.
- Refer to: *Lining the Vest, Method 1,* page 17 .

Hand Quilting and Sashiko

General Quilting Instructions

All of the vests require some handwork whether it be the hand-quilting around the edges of the garment or the entire vest. I think a little handwork goes a long way and should be incorporated whenever possible. I really like to use Perle cotton, size 8, for the hand-stitching around the edges. The stitches can be longer and it will still look good. This size Perle cotton works really well for all the Sashiko designs and any quilting where you want to emphasize the design. Use regular thread and beeswax where you want the fine hand-quilted look.

MARKING THE DESIGN

Once you have chosen your design, trace the design onto white paper. Go over the design with a black, permanent marker. Place the design under the outer fabric, pattern right-side up and fabric right-side up. Trace the design onto the fabric using the marking tool of your choice. Mark as lightly as possible—just so you can barely see the marks. You'll be surprised how much really shows. (You did pre-test your marking tool?)

Occasionally, you can't see through the fabric. Use a light source—a window, a lamp under a sheet of glass, or a light table.

BASTING

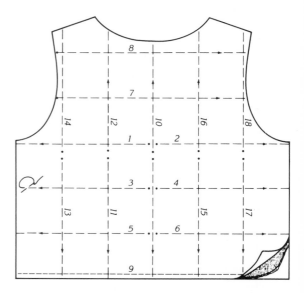

Hand-baste the outer fabric to the batting. Use white thread and baste from the center out, horizontally and vertically, to form a 3″ (7.6 cm) grid. Some adept people do not baste as much as I do, but I feel that the more you baste, the easier it is to quilt. One of my best quilters safety pins her work, but she is really good. Use whatever method you prefer, but if you are a beginner, baste.

HAND QUILTING

Hand-quilting is really fun! I don't know exactly why—it's time consuming and needs to be done fairly well. I suppose it is fun because it is therapeutic, rewarding, quiet, personally addictive, and amazing that we can even find the time for it in our busy schedules. Quilting is the kind of thing that once you try it, you will somehow find the time for it again and again. Quilting is a running stitch that usually catches three layers together into a textile sandwich. Most of the vests in this book tell you to quilt through the outer fabric and the batting only. This will give you a flatter look, which is probably better in the long run, and it also makes the lining process easier.

You should have three stitching objectives while quilting:

1) Straight stitches.

2) Even stitches on the top, that is, the same amount of fabric between the stitches as the stitch length showing.

3) Short stitches, which will come with practice and will depend on the thickness of the fabric and batting.

QUILTING PROCESS

• Thread the needle. Cut the thread about 18″ (45.7 cm) long. Tie a single knot on the end you cut. A big, rolled knot, or a "waste knot," will wear a hole in your fabric. Wax the thread with beeswax; this will help the thread pull through more easily. Start by coming through the fabric from the batting side. (If you are going through all three layers, gently tug on the knot and pop it through the top layer so the knot will be hidden.)

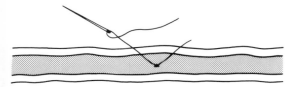

Bring the needle through to a marked line. Begin by taking one or two short, even running stitches. Pull on your threaded needle, slightly tugging so that the stitches sink into the surface.

• Continue quilting until you get to the end of your thread, or until you reach the end of the design.

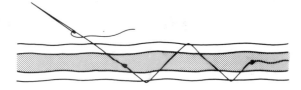

• Form a single knot close to the surface of the top fabric before you sew your last stitch. Place the needle through the top layer and bring it out on top again about ½″ (12 mm) away from where you took the last stitch on the top of the vest.

• Slightly tug on the knot, popping it between the layers. If you are not quilting through a lining, just knot on the batting side.

• Quilt the entire vest on the quilting lines. When quilting, be careful not to quilt through or split the basting threads.

• Remove the basting threads and admire.

• Refer to your vest for the finishing method.

Sashiko

Ann West and Sondra Rudey have created a number of vests using Sashiko designs. A Sashiko design is created by the use of a heavy thread and a running stitch to create an embellishment on cloth.

This decorative stitchery was used in Japan on field clothing. Lately, with the help of a new book, *Sashiko,* by Kimi Ota, this look can be achieved by a beginner. It is especially adaptable for the junior vest—it has the desired beauty but is not too obvious.

These Sashiko vests are some of the easiest in the book. You can use the designs here, or any other suitable design you prefer.

Choose your design. Take a moment or two and study the design. It is probably symmetrical and straightforward. Are the designs for the fronts reversed?

I have designed all of these vests so that you may use the center back line to begin the placement of your design.

BACK AND FRONTS

- Cut out the outer vest fabric. Mark the center back line.
- Trace the template onto plastic, using a Sharpie pen.
- Cut out the plastic template, including the notches if any. Place the template on the center back line on the bottom and trace around it. Use a drafting pencil or any fine light marking pencil.
- Mark the designs as indicated for your view.
- Baste the outer back and front fabrics to the batting, using white thread. Baste horizontally and vertically every three inches (7.6 cm). Refer to: *Hand Quilting,* page 78.
- Quilt or "Sashiko" the designs.

In Sashiko, you will try to sew the longest lines or "routes" from edge to edge without stopping or starting. Study each design. Notice that there are stitching paths indicated.

Materials:

Plain Fabric	CHILD 2–8	JUNIOR 5–9	ADULT 8–14	ADULT 16–22
Outer vest	½ yd (.46 m)	¾ yd (.7 m)	¾ yd (.7 m)	1½ yd (1.4 m)
Lining	½ yd (.46 m)	¾ yd (.7 m)	¾ yd (.7 m)	1½ yd (1.4 m)
Batting	½ yd (.46 m)	¾ yd (.7 m)	¾ yd (.7 m)	1½ yd (1.4 m)
Fabric for cording (if desired)	½ yd (.46 m)	½ yd (.46 m)	½ yd (.46 m)	¾ yd (.7 m)
Size #16 cord	2 yd (1.8 m)	3 yd (2.7 m)	4 yd (3.65 m)	5 yd (4.57 m)
Contrast Fabric	½ yd (.46 m)	½ yd (.46 m)	¾ yd (.7 m)	¾ yd (.7 m)
Batting, thin	½ yd (.46 m)	¾ yd (.7 m)	¾ yd (.7 m)	1½ yd (1.4 m)

NOTIONS: #8 Perle cotton to match or contrast; #8 Crewel needle; C-Thru® B-85 ruler; water-soluble pen; pencil; 1 spool matching thread; 4 buttons; plastic for templates; white thread for basting; beeswax.

REFER TO:
1) Fabric Preparation, page 10.
2) Making and Fitting the Trial Vest, page 12.
3) Hand Quilting, page 78.
4) Lining the Vest, Method 1, page 17.

To determine how long your thread needs to be to sew the long continuous line, just lay the thread over the marked line in the direction you are going to stitch. Cut the thread 4″ (10.1 cm) or so longer than this measurement. Use beeswax on the Perle cotton for easier stitching. Stitch your designs, remove the bastings. Refer to: *Lining the Vest, Method 1,* page 17.

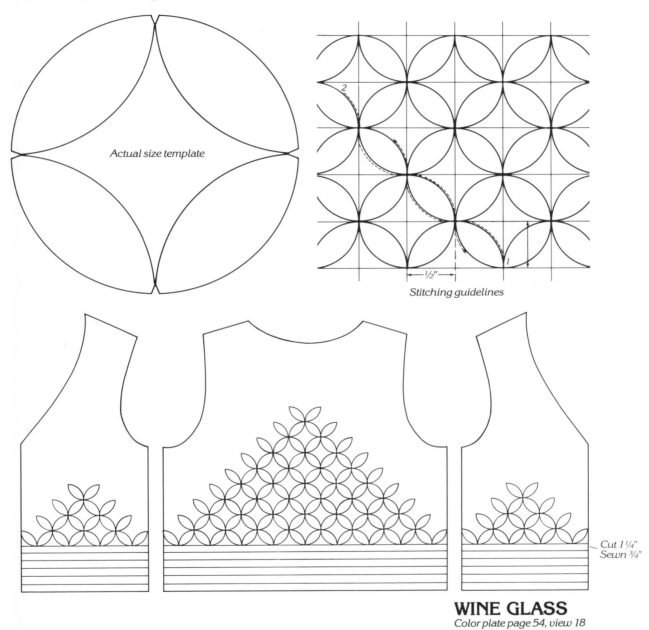

Actual size template

Stitching guidelines

WINE GLASS
Color plate page 54, view 18

~ *Cut 1¼″*
Sewn ¾″

POINTED BLUE OCEAN WAVES
Color plate page 55, view 21

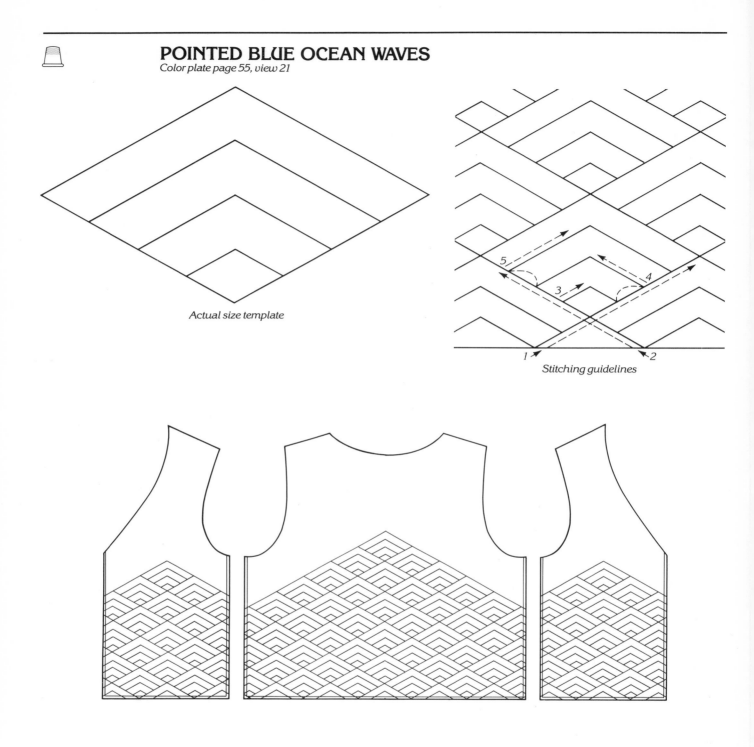

Actual size template

Stitching guidelines

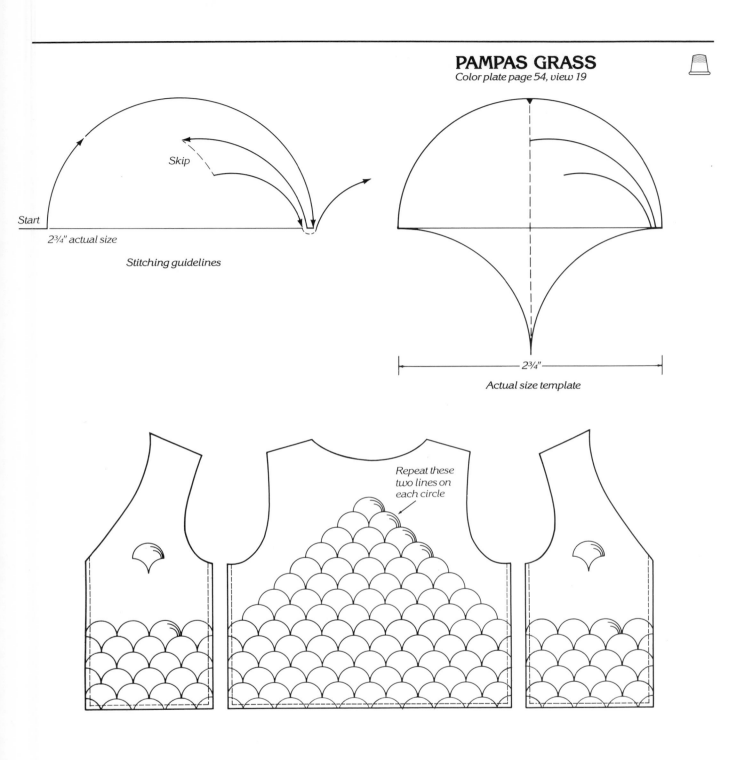

Start

Skip

2¾" actual size

Stitching guidelines

2¾"

Actual size template

Repeat these two lines on each circle

CHRISTMAS TREES
Color plate page 55, view 23

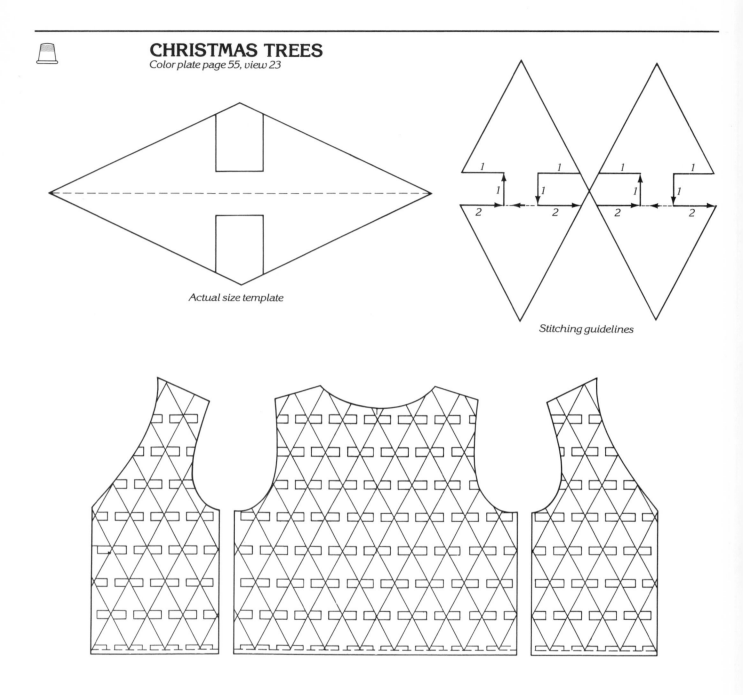

Actual size template

Stitching guidelines

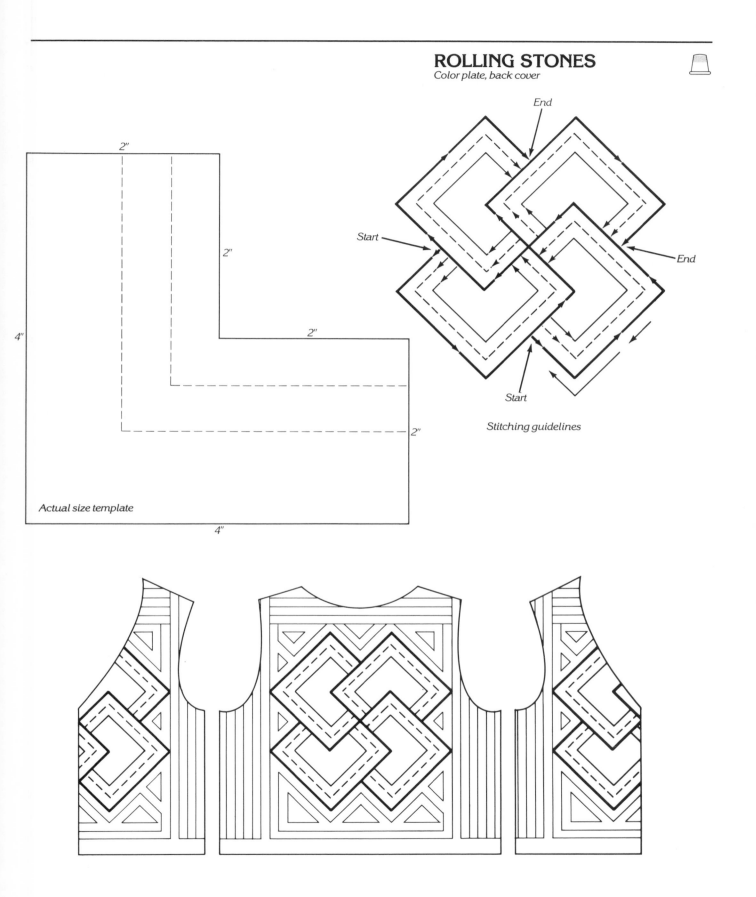

End

Start

End

Start

Stitching guidelines

2"

2"

2"

4"

2"

4"

Actual size template

LILIES
Color plate, back cover

Draw designs on the vest fabric, Refer to Hand Quilting, line the vest using Method 1.

A Note On Creativity

What can I say without starting another book. Flat out, every one has some creative forces within which are just asking for some encouragement to surface.

I am often asked, "How do you really work?" Well, it's easy for me. First of all, I'm not at all afraid of making mistakes or tossing something out. Second, the most important part of the creative process is the working out of the problem, not the finished product. Often times I will decide to tackle some particular problem, be it accurate seams, using an unusual design or a far-out fabric. I will spend many hours of work and thought resolving the situation never to worry about finishing. I think that lack of worry about finishing is what frees me to work. This is not to say that I never finish anything. I just finish the most important things.

Well, this method is great if you have the time and fabric to play around with. But what about those of you who are the finishers? Without you I couldn't create or write. Only because of you, the reader and the finishers in this world, can the artist or the author have the luxury of a studio. This book became my studio for the last six months. It is for you.

Begin with a thought, or a thing that you love.

Be it a design, a fabric or whatever, just know that all of the vests in this book were simply created. They all began from a single thought or source, maybe it was a fabric or a ribbon or a block which was made and never used.

I am including here the format or the outline for you to use to create your own vest. The idea is to break up the format into horizontal or vertical areas, piece the fabric, fill these areas, and embellish the vest by incorporating your inspiration.

Sondra had decided to create a vest-a-month around a theme for each month. In February she made her first Sashiko vest, page 54, which opened her mind to all sorts of creative stitchery. Sondra chose the Shamrock theme for March (the designs came from *The Finishing Touch*).

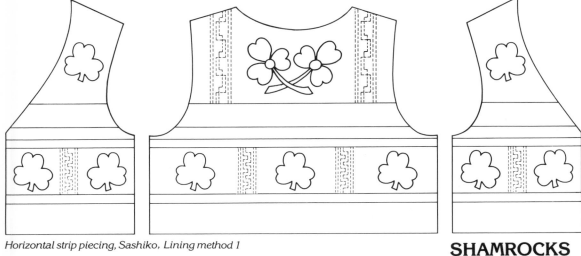

Horizontal strip piecing, Sashiko, Lining method 1

SHAMROCKS
Color plate page 54, view 17

- **Use the following diagram for your design area.**
- Divide the vest into fabric areas. Sketch your designs into the areas. Make pattern pieces by overlaying pattern paper. Add the seam allowance to the new patterns. Cut two patterns if necessary to reverse the designs that need to be mirrored.
- Sew the smallest pieces together to create horizontal or vertical strips.

- Mark any quilting or stitchery lines lightly on the fabric.
- Assemble the fabric to fill the batting.
- Baste the fabric to the batting.
- Stitch or embellish as desired.
- Trim the vest and line it using Method 1 or any method which seems best. If you have progressed this far, you pretty well really do not need any more advice, just time to sew.

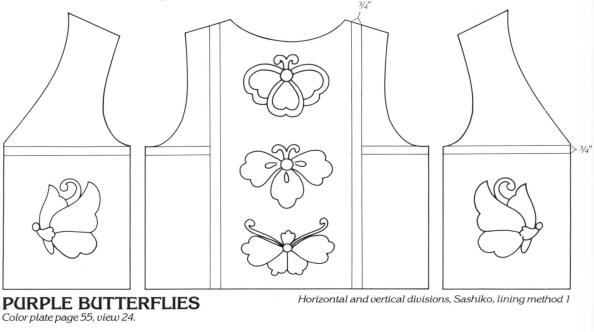

PURPLE BUTTERFLIES
Color plate page 55, view 24.

Horizontal and vertical divisions, Sashiko, lining method 1

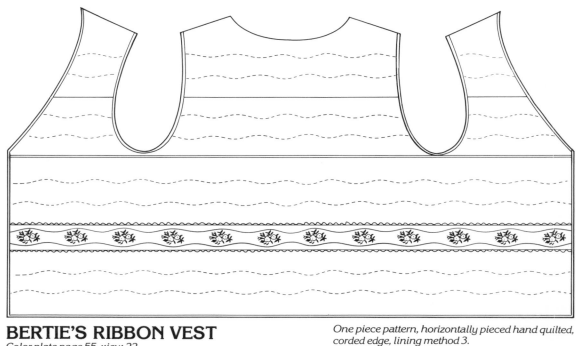

BERTIE'S RIBBON VEST
Color plate page 55, view 22

One piece pattern, horizontally pieced hand quilted, corded edge, lining method 3.

Machine Applique and Quilting

Machine Applique

Machine applique may be used to create the major portion of the design, or it may be used as an added touch in combination with other techniques.

In order to achieve really fine machine applique, I recommend that you make a practice block.

PRACTICE BLOCK

Materials

One 4" (10 cm²) square background fabric
One 4" (10 cm²) square applique fabric
One 4" (10 cm²) square tear-away paper stabilizer
One 4" (10 cm²) square lightweight fusible interfacing
Marking tool (Sharpie Fine-line marker, black only)
Machine embroidery thread
Fabric glue stick
Scissors
Iron
Open toe foot

SETTING THE MACHINE FOR APPLIQUE

Checkpoints:
- Check the tension in the bobbin case. The thread should pull more to the tight side than loose.
- Loosen the top tension to 2.5 (5 is normal). The top tension should be loose so that the upper thread is pulled to the underside of the fabric.
- Put a new needle in the machine. I recommend a size 10/11 to 14 (70–90). The smaller the number the finer the needle.
- Use machine embroidery thread on the top (or any well made, fine thread).
- Fill the bobbin with a contrasting thread. I use a contrasting thread on the bobbin for the test, then I change to a matching thread for the actual applique.
- Use an open toe foot.

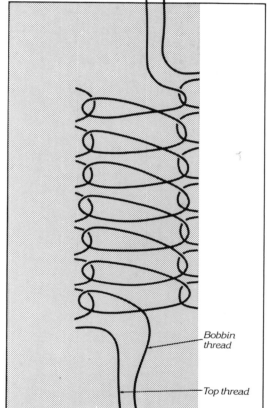

The top thread will wrap to the back
Back of test fabric

Bobbin thread

Top thread

- Set stitch width to medium, 2.5 to 3.0. The stitch width can be varied to whatever looks nice, or whatever you decide is needed. The width will depend on how large the applique pieces are and how wide you want the satin stitch to appear.
- Set the stitch length as close to 0 as you can without having the machine sew in place. Don't begin at 0 and move away from it as the machine will jam. It is safer to move the length adjustment toward 0, bringing the distance between the stitches closer and closer. Sew a row of stitches on the side of the test fabric to see what is happening. Because you've loosened the top tension, the thread should wrap to the back, which will be normal for all machine applique.

FUSING THE APPLIQUE FABRIC

- Place a 4″ (10 cm²) square of lightweight fusible interfacing, beady side up, over the tulip pattern, Fig. a.
- Trace the tulip with a marking tool that will show up when you turn the fusible over. We have tried every type of marking tool and I am going to recommend a Fine-line Sharpie Permanent pen, *black* only. This is unheard of in a quilt book, so don't tell anyone. Please test your markers with a hot iron and a damp cloth.
  I mark slightly outside the pattern line so that when I cut out the fused fabric I cut the marked line away. Mark carefully.

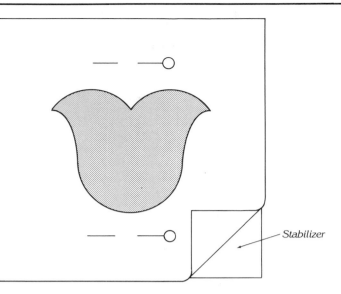

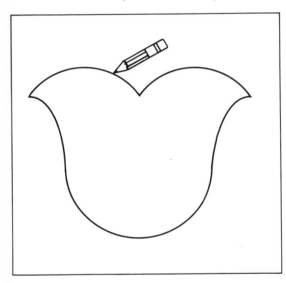

- Pin a 4″ (10 cm²) square of tear-away stabilizer behind the background fabric.

- Fuse the interfacing, beady side down, to the wrong side of the tulip fabric.
  (Use a damp pressing cloth over the fusible with the iron set on "wool." Press for ten seconds. Let the fabric cool before handling. Cut out the tulip just inside your marked lines.
- Use sharp scissors and cut carefully.

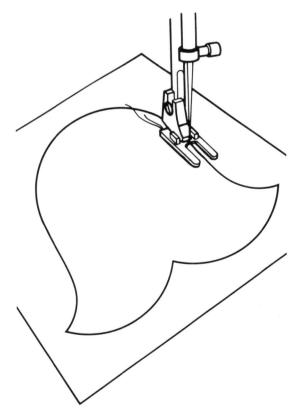

- Place a continuous bead of fabric glue stick around the edge of the fused side of the tulip. Position the tulip, gluey side down, in the center of the 4″ (10 cm²) background fabric.

- Begin on the right side of the tulip.
- Bring the bobbin thread to the top. Hold both threads to one side, under the presser foot.
- Check the swing of the needle to see that the needle swings to the right just to cover the edge of the applique.

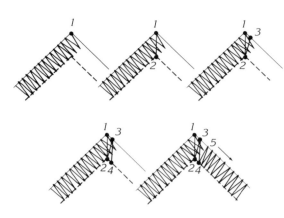

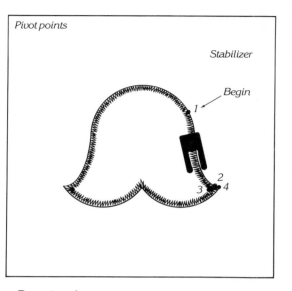

- Sew to the first point; leave the needle in the fabric ON THE OUTSIDE FOR AN OUTSIDE TURN. Lift the presser bar and turn the fabric toward you.

NOTE: If you can taper your stitch width while zig-zagging you might wish to do some practice tapering to the points.

- Hand-pivot, following the diagram, for a perfect point.
- Zig-zag until you reach the V.
- Zig-zag five stitches past the V on the tulip fabric or equal to the width of your satin stitch.
- LEAVE THE NEEDLE ON THE INSIDE FOR AN INSIDE TURN. (On the left side.)

- Lift the presser bar and pivot as shown for a perfect inside pivot.
- Continue around the tulip.

- Practice the pivot points.
- On the curves you will have to pivot often.
- Pull the threads to the back and tie.
- Tear away the stabilizer.

It is definitely worth your while to practice. When you feel comfortable with this technique, go on to your vest.

Successful Machine Applique, published by Yours Truly, Inc., is an excellent resource. A note on machine applique: I am aware of four or five different methods of machine applique, each having their advantages and disadvantages. This method is the one we teach in my shop on all brands of machines. It seems to be the most universal. Also, we have found that since every machine will vary, so will the application. There are other successful approaches. You will learn to do whatever is most applicable to your own situation.

NOTE: I found that if I drew four or five tulips onto a scrap of fabric, placed a piece of stabilizer between the fabric and the feed dog, and practiced my points, I really observed what I was doing. Pivot points may be discussed at length but until you really try it, it won't mean anything.

The open toe foot makes all the difference too.

Lotus Blossom

Color plate page 56, view 25

Materials

	Child 2–8	Junior 5–9	Adult 8–14	Adult 16–22
A Diamond	¼ yd (.23 m)	¼ yd (.23 m)	¼ yd (.23 m)	¼ yd (.23 m)
B Stem	¼ yd (.23 m)	¼ yd (.23 m)	¼ yd (.23 m)	¼ yd (.23 m)
C Leaves	⅛ yd (.11 m)	⅛ yd (.11 m)	⅛ yd (.11 m)	⅛ yd (.11 m)
D Outer petal	¼ yd (.23 m)	¼ yd (.23 m)	¼ yd (.23 m)	¼ yd (.23 m)
E Inner petal	¼ yd (.23 m)	¼ yd (.23 m)	¼ yd (.23 m)	¼ yd (.23 m)
F Centers	¼ yd (.23 m)	¼ yd (.23 m)	¼ yd (.23 m)	¼ yd (.23 m)
G Outer Vest Fabric	½ yd (.46 m)	¾ yd (.7 m)	¾ yd (.7 m)	1½ yd (1.4 m)
Lining	½ yd (.46 m)	¾ yd (.7 m)	¾ yd (.7 m)	1½ yd (1.4 m)
Batting	½ yd (.46 m)	¾ yd (.7 m)	¾ yd (.7 m)	1½ yd (1.4 m)

NOTIONS: Fabric glue stick; sewing machine needles #70 (11); machine embroidery thread to match each fabric; open toe foot; ½ yard (.46 m) lightweight fusible interfacing; 1 yard (91.4 m) tear away stabilizer; one spool thread to match outer fabric; #8 Perle cotton for quilting; #8 Crewel needle; Sharpie Fine-line marker (black only); large white paper.

REFER TO:
1) Fabric Preparation, page 10.
2) Making and Fitting the Trial Vest, page 12.
3) Machine Applique Practice Block, page 90.
4) Hand Quilting, page 78.
5) Lining the Vest, Method 1, page 17.

Jenny Gardella adapted this design from *F is for Flowers,* by Ellen Mosbarger. All of Ellen's books are excellent sources for machine applique designs.

Jenny's machine applique is among the finest I have ever seen. This particular design is a little intricate, so a little practice will go a long way. Please take a moment and make the practice block, page 90. It will be very worth your while.

VEST BACK

Cut out the outer vest back fabric.

Preparing the Outer Fabric for Machine Applique

- Place a large sheet of white paper over the full-size pattern and trace it with a permanent felt marker (Sharpie), page 95.
- Place the outer vest fabric over the design.
- Center the design.
- *Lightly* trace the pattern onto the fabric for applique placement. You may have to use a window or a light table to trace.

Preparing the Fusible

- Place a sheet of fusible (beady side up) over the design. Trace each applique pattern piece individually—move the fusible over an inch or so each time before tracing another pattern piece.

Fusing the Fabric

- Following the diagrams, fuse the interfacing according to the manufacturer's directions. If not available, place the fusible beady side down on the wrong side of the fabric, place a damp cloth or damp paper towel on top of the fusible (Jenny keeps a spray bottle of water handy), and iron for fifteen seconds with iron set on steam or wool. Allow fabric to cool before handling.
- Cut out the individual pieces exactly on the marked line (or slightly inside to eliminate the markings).
- Begin with design for fabric A (diamond). Trace four of the pattern pieces for the diamond adding ¼″ (6 mm) seam allowance to *ends* only, and reversing two of them if necessary. (If you are using a stripe or one-way design, you will need to reverse two sections for the left side.)
- Continue tracing until you have *all* the applique parts marked on the beady side of the fusible.
- Check to make sure you can see the design on the non-beady side; re-trace if necessary.

Piecing the Diamond

- Sew the two parts for the left side together.
- Sew the two parts for the right side together.
- Press the seam open and trim.
- Place the two sewn halves over your marked design for a final check before you sew the top and bottom.
- Sew the top and the bottom seams at ¼″ (6 mm).
- Press the seams open. Trim seam allowances.

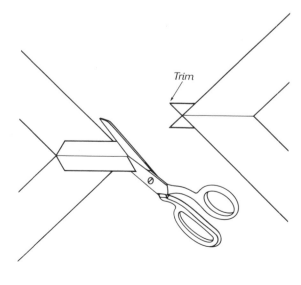

Trim

Lavender

Blue

White

Light
Green

Light
Green

Light
Green

Lavender

Blue

Lavender

White

Light
Green

Blue

Light
Green

Light
Green

Dark
Green

Light
Green

Light
Green

Light
Green

95

Preparation for Applique On the Back

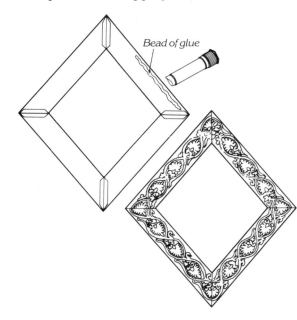

Bead of glue

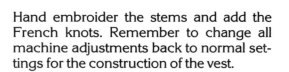

- Place a continuous coating of fabric glue stick around all the inner and outer edges of the diamond.
- Turn the diamond over and position it on your marked lines on the vest back.
- Glue each part down, beginning with the one closest to the background, i.e., the white flower centers, next the lavender, then the blue, the green, etc.
- Good time to take a break! Go wash up! 'Cuz when you get back, you're going to finish your applique.

MACHINE APPLIQUE
(After practice block)
- Fill the bobbin with thread to match the diamond fabric. You will applique the fabric closest to the background fabric first, the diamond.
- Pin an 11″ by 14″ (28 x 35 cm) piece of tear-away stabilizer between the background fabric and the feed dog.
- Applique the diamond; inside edge first, then outside edge.
- Change the thread on the top to match the white flower centers. Continue appliqueing until all is finished.
- Pull the threads to the back, tie off and clip.
- Remove the tear-away-stabilizer.
- Press if needed. (I place a terry towel on the ironing board and use a cloth over the top to absorb the thickness of the applique.) Stand back and admire your work! You may now applique just about anything you wish.

Hand embroider the stems and add the French knots. Remember to change all machine adjustments back to normal settings for the construction of the vest.

CONSTRUCTION AND FINISHING THE VEST
Marking the quilting designs:
- Cut out two vest fronts.
- Place the right front over the Lotus Blossom design and trace the design onto the fabric. For quilting mark light lines that you can barely see.
- Reverse the design for the left front and trace.
- Mark the vertical quilting lines 2″ (5 cm) apart beginning at the center. (I marked half circles along the bottom edge using a canning jar lid for a template.)
- Mark vertical quilting lines on the back, 2″ (5 cm) apart, center out.
- Quilt the vest (I used #8 Perle cotton).
  Refer to: *Hand Quilting,* page 78.
- Trim the vest to the original pattern.
- Baste the outer vest to the batting as shown in diagram.
  Refer to: *Lining the Vest, Method 1,* page 17.

Art Nouveau

Color plate page 56, view 26

Materials

	ADULT 8–12	ADULT 14–22
Vest Fabric (solid)	¾ yd (.7 m)	1½ yd (1.4 m)
Batting	¾ yd (.7 m)	1½ yd (1.4 m)
Lining	¾ yd (.7 m)	1½ yd (1.4 m)
Green Stems, Leaves	⅜ yd (.34 m)	⅜ yd (.34 m)
Flowers solid	¼ yd (.23 m)	¼ yd (.23 m)
Flowers Stripe (May be the same as the lining)	¼ yd (.23 m)	¼ yd (.23 m)

NOTIONS: 1 yard (91.4 m) lightweight, fusible iron-on interfacing; 1 yard (91.4 m) tear-away-stabilizer; fabric glue stick; thread to match vest fabric; thread to match each fabric of the applique, large sheets of white paper for tracing the pattern; scissors; permanent marker (Sharpie Fine-line, black only); iron; pressing cloth; open toe foot.

REFER TO:
1) Fabric Preparation, page 10.
2) Making and Fitting the Trial Vest, page 12.
3) Machine Applique Practice block, page 90.
4) Machine Quilting, page 101.
5) Lining the Vest, Method 1, page 17.

Eunice Roberts created this elegant vest. She was inspired by Philomena Wiechec's book, *Celtic Quilt Designs.* The really unique feature of this vest is that Eunice created the flower centers by pleating a narrow striped fabric. The entire design was machine appliqued and machine quilted.

You may use the "Marmie" method of making bias as suggested in Philomena's book.

Cut bias strips 1¼″ wide. Fold the bias in half, right side out. Sew a little more than ¼″ from the fold the length of the bias. Trim the seam allowance. Place the Bias Bar inside the bias. Roll the seam to the back of the bar and press. Position and pin the bias on the marked lines. Hand or machine applique in place.

PREPARING THE BACK
FOR MACHINE APPLIQUE

- Trace the entire applique design onto a large sheet of white paper.
- Center the outer vest fabric over the design and trace lightly.

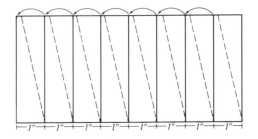

- 1 strip plain fabric or fabric with stripe design which repeats approximately every inch. If plain, mark as indicated above. If striped, use striped design for the markers, fold, bringing the unbroken line to the dotted line, and press. Scallop the outer edge by trimming into pleat.

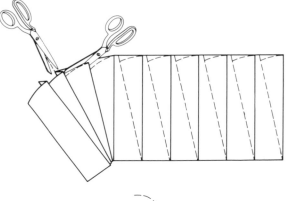

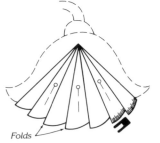

Folds

- Applique in place using a stretch hemming stitch with the length set close to 0. Do a little practice on a test pleated fabric. If your machine does not have a stretch hem stitch, just applique with the stitch width set on 4 and the length near 0.

  Preparing applique parts:
- Trace all the parts for the applique onto beady side of fusible interfacing, leaving at least 1" (2.5 cm) between parts.

- Trace around all the stem and leaf parts onto the green fabric. Trace all appliques onto corresponding fabrics. Refer to: *Machine Applique Practice Block,* page 90.
- Fuse your parts, cut them out and glue to back.
- Machine applique all of the parts.
- Tear away the stabilizer on the back.
- Press if needed.
- Bring loose threads to the back and tie.
- Applique a part of the design onto the right front, if desired. Use patterns.
- Mark the outer fabric for machine quilting.

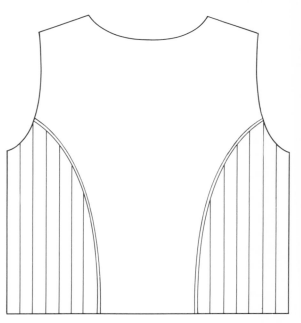

- Draw a curved line from the back armholes to the bottom.
- Draw another line 1/4" (6 mm) in from that line.
- Mark straight lines from the top of the curve to the bottom of the vest, every 1" (2.5 cm)
- Mark vertical rows on the fronts every 1" (2.5 cm).
- Baste outer fabric to batting, page 101.
- Machine quilt on these lines, using a dual feed foot. Refer to: *Machine Quilting,* page 102.
- Use the quilting guide for straight lines.
- Refer to: *Lining the Vest, Method 1,* page 17.

Bertie's Rainbow

MACHINE QUILTING

There are two or three different techniques that can be used in combination or by themselves to quickly produce a machine quilted vest.

Bertie used the rainbow panel to create a striking and efficiently produced vest. She eliminated the side seams from the pattern so that she could use the full size panel making a one piece vest. She used the walking foot to machine quilt the fabric.

I decided that I had better try one, in order to write about it. I used the walking foot on the curves of the rainbow, then I removed the foot, lowered the feed dog and hand guided the panel wherever there were curvy lines. Then I attached the quilting guide and used this guide to sew parallel lines above and below the rainbow. I decided this was too much stopping and starting, even though it only took me an hour or so.

When Sondra's daughter, Kitzi signed up for our young people's class last week I encouraged her to make a vest using this panel.

Now, she is a new sewer, I couldn't give her a list of techniques seven miles long. I wanted to see her finish.

I told Kitzi to quilt the entire panel, after basting it really well, with just the walking foot. She did it, beautifully! So, what I am saying, again, yes there are known different methods. Find the one that is best for you.

Cut one twelve inch square of fabric and batting and inner-lining, draw some practice lines on the fabric, baste the squares together and practice.

QUILTING THE FABRIC

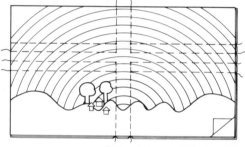

Color plate page 56, view 27

- Baste the panel, batting and inner-lining together. Baste every three inches apart horizontally and vertically from the center out. (The basting threads may get in your way when you sew over them. You may clip the bastings as you sew to them.)

Materials

	JUNIORS 5–9	ADULTS 8–20
Panel or fabric 27″ by 45″ (.7 x 1.15 m)	1 yd (.91 m)	1 yd (.91 m)
Batting	¾ yd (.7 m)	¾ yd (.7 m)
Inner lining	¾ yd (.7 m)	¾ yd (.7 m)
Lining	¾ yd (.7 m)	¾ yd (.7 m)

NOTIONS: Thread to match each color; walking foot; open toe foot; quilting foot; white thread for basting.

REFER TO:
1) Making and Fitting the Trial Vest, page 12.
2) Lining The Vest, Method 3, page 27.

- Put the Walking Foot on the machine.
- Use a thread that matches the bottom ray of the rainbow.

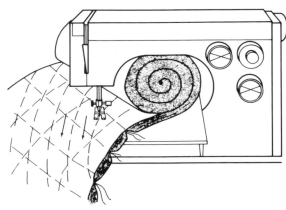

- Roll the fabric so that it will fit in the open area of the machine.
  (You will have to keep rolling, and un-rolling the fabric as you sew.)
- Sew the bottom ray, from the center out, toward you.
- Go back and sew the next row up, center out, toward you. (Sew as many rows as you can that the thread matches.)
- Without changing thread, go back to the bottom ray and sew out in the other direction. Continue, until you need to change threads.
- Change threads as needed and finish the quilting from the center out each time.
- Quilt around the curvy lines, one of two methods. Leave the walking foot on and lift the presser bar whenever you need to turn, or remove the foot, lower the feed dog and hand guide the fabric under the needle. (See *Machine Embroidery Practice Block*, page 90.)
- Remove the basting threads. Pull all of the threads to the back and tie.
- Trace the pattern for your size onto large paper. Place the pattern pieces together at the side seams. Eliminate the side seams by overlapping the seam lines one inch (2.5 cm) and tape the paper together.

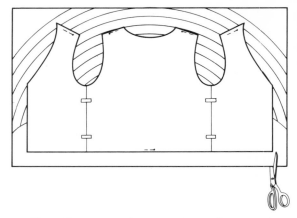

- Use the one-piece pattern for cutting placement on your quilted panel.
- Move the pattern around over the fabric until you have as much of the scene as you can behind the pattern.

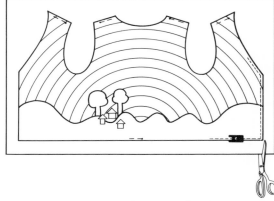

- Pin the pattern and cut out the vest.
- Stay stitch around the arm-holes ½" (12 mm) from the edge.
- Stay stitch around the entire vest a little less than ½" (12 mm).
- Use your trimmed vest for the pattern to cut out the lining.
- Pin the vest to the lining, right sides together.
- Cut out the lining.
- Stay stitch around the lining arm-holes, ½" (12 mm) from the edge. It is almost finished. Refer to: *Lining the Vest, Method 3*, page 27.

Bibliography

BRADKIN, CHERYL GREIDER. *The Seminole Patchwork Book.* Yours Truly, Inc., Atlanta, GA 1979.

FANNING, ROBBIE AND TONY. *The Complete Book of Machine Quilting.* Chilton Book Company, Randor, PA, 1980.

LAURY, JEAN RAY. *Quilted Clothing.* Oxmoor House, Inc., Birmingham, AL, 1982.

LEE, BARBARA. *Successful Machine Applique.* Yours Truly, Inc., Atlanta, GA, 1978.

LEMAN, BONNIE AND MARTIN, JUDY. *Taking the Math Out of Making Patchwork Quilts.* M.Q.M. Publishing Co., 67 W. 44th Wheatridge, Denver, CO 80033, 1981.

LEONE, DIANA. *The Sampler Quilt.* 2721 Lyle Court, Santa Clara, CA 95051, 1980.

MOSBARGER, ELLEN. *A Is For Applique.* Calico Mouse Publications, 924 Sespe Ave., W. Fillmore, CA 93015, 1980.

MOSBARGER, ELLEN. *P Is For Patterns.* Calico Mouse Publications, 924 Sespe Ave., W. Fillmore, CA 93015, 1981.

MOSBARGER, ELLEN. *F Is For Flowers.* Calico Mouse Publications, 924 Sespe Ave., W. Fillmore, CA 93015, 1981.

MOSBARGER, ELLEN. *V Is For Victorian.* Calico Mouse Publicatioins, 924 Sespe Ave., W. Fillmore, CA 93015, 1981.

OTA, KIMI. *Sashiko Quilting.* 10300 61st Avenue So., Seattle, WA 98178, 1981.

THOMPSON, SHIRLEY. *The Finishing Touch.* Powell Publications, PO Box 513, Edmonds, WA 98020, 1981.

WIECHEC, PHILOMENA. *Celtic Quilt Designs.* 19170 Portos Drive, Saratoga, CA 95070, 1980.

YOUNG, BLANCHE AND HELEN. *Trip Around the World Quilts.* Box 925, Oak View, CA 93022, 1980.

About the Author

Diana Leone, owner of The Quilting Bee of Los Altos, California has been involved in the quilt world for the past twelve years. She has designed many award-winning quilts, lectured throughout the United States, Canada and Japan. She teaches, writes and owns a publishing company.

A graduate from San Jose State University with a BA and MA in Art Education, Diana has taught quiltmaking and art at San Jose State and at the high school level prior to owning her own business.